Building Self-Esteem in Teens

Accept Who You Are, Manage Emotions, Become Self-Confident, and Accomplish Your Goals to Be the Person You Want to Be

Scott Douglas

Table of Contents

Introduction

Never bend your head. Always hold it high. Look the world straight in the eye. –
Helen Keller (In T. Gur, *Never Bend Your Head*)

Confidence can be an important weapon, and all the successful people since the beginning of time know how to wield it. Self-confidence comes from your perception of yourself and your "self-belief," and it can be defined "as a feeling of trust in one's abilities, qualities, and judgement" (Norton, 2018). When you find your self-confidence, you will find a whole new world, and it all starts with working on your self-esteem.

I once knew a kid who struggled with his self-esteem and had no confidence at all. He'd wake up every day and take a look in the mirror, hating what he'd see. His appearance, what his voice sounded like, his entire personality—he hated everything. He felt powerless and was miserable. If he laughed, it was for just a moment, then he'd remember that he truly hated the way his laugh sounded. If he was happy for just one second, he'd remember that he didn't deserve it. He couldn't accept any compliments and when someone did have something nice to say about him, he somehow found a way to dismiss it. I'd watch him get bullied because he just wouldn't fight for himself, through words or otherwise. He constantly worried and put himself down. He was hurtling toward a very dark place where nothing in the world could help him.

One day, I shared some of my most valuable strategies with him, which he quietly accepted, and I never saw him for a long time. When I finally met him again recently, he was a completely different person. The first thing I noticed was that he had the biggest smile on his face and his entire demeanor had changed. Even though he went through the toughest time back then, he was a thriving, confident person now. Unbeknownst to me, he had taken everything I had offered him and implemented it steadfastly in his life. His story of resilience and strength in the face of challenges is incredible, and his gratitude was humbling.

If you're a teenager like him who has felt self-doubt weighing you down for as long as you can remember, and you just want the feeling of confidence so you can be happier, more carefree, and have the ability to chase your dreams, then this book is going to be a game-changer. This isn't just any other ordinary self-help book. This is going to be your companion and mentor as you take the journey to the well-deserved freedom you're looking for. This book has a unique and holistic approach that will bridge the role of parents and children in the development of self-esteem.

This book will have a seven-step framework and practical guide that will help parents and teens to understand what they're going through, and combat it effectively. This is your comprehensive roadmap with everything you need to guide you through the journey of enriching your self-esteem. If you struggle with body image issues, academic pressure, bullying, peer pressure, expectations from your parents, or perfectionist tendencies, you will find strategies you can use to improve your life.

Once you have mastered the seven-step road map, you will have developed important skills such as being aware of yourself, through understanding your emotions, actions, and relationships. You will develop self-awareness, which is an important foundation to build self-esteem. Cultivating self-awareness will teach you how to love yourself, regardless of what you look like or what society says you should be. Nothing will stand in your way of being self-compassionate and learning to be kind and gentle with yourself. You will be a master of destroying self-criticism and negative self-talk, and you will learn how to motivate yourself. You will learn the crucial steps toward emotional resilience so that you can accept change and cope with any stressful event that happens in your life.

Self-acceptance will become second nature to you. Your self-worth will increase, allowing you to gain confidence in your abilities. You will feel good about yourself holistically. One of the most important steps in the framework is learning to cultivate healthy relationships, which will guide and teach you everything that you need to know about improving your relationships and turning the unhealthy ones into ones that are good for you. You will learn some important strategies and tips for conflict resolution and communication, such as how to set boundaries that are important for your mental health and learning to be empathetic. The most important step that you will learn is to stand up for yourself. You will discover strategies to deal with peer pressure and bullying, and techniques to help you change your perspective and stand up for yourself.

Are you a parent who can see the pain in your kid's eyes every day? You can probably already see what their low self-esteem is doing to their life, and you can already see that their lack of self-worth is affecting their relationships negatively. Their school life probably isn't going very well, they seem unhappy more often than not, and they just seem unhappy in general. This is your chance for empowerment and motivation. This might seem like a mammoth task—huge and impossible—but with the strategies and tips in this book, you will find a path that's simple and effective.

You will discover the way to unlock your self-confidence and improve your self-esteem. You will find everything you need to know about recognizing the signs and symptoms of low self-esteem, a breakdown of its causes, what issues to look out for, and most importantly, you will discover how to fight it to give your child the happy and healthy life they need. It's going to be an amazing feeling when you see the confidence in their body language, their new ability to take positive risks, and getting out of their comfort zone. They will be calmer, more focused, and achieve what they set out to do. Here's to a beautiful journey through breaking free of low self-esteem, accepting who you are, learning to manage your emotions, becoming self-confident, and accomplishing your goals. You can do this!

As soon as you trust yourself, you will know how to live. –Johann Wolfgang von Goethe

Trusting yourself is a significant aspect of conquering self-esteem, and to get there, you need to first have a comprehensive understanding of the idea behind self-esteem and the role that it plays in your personal development. Self-esteem will carry you through all of life's challenges, and it is the basis of who you are and your sense of self. If you understand self-esteem, you will be able to learn how to be more self-assured, which is a critical aspect of being able to function to your fullest potential. This chapter lays out this important concept and its influence on who you are, how you see yourself, and the world around you. We will dive into the psychology behind self-esteem and what it is at its very core to pave the way toward learning the strategies to improve it.

What Is Self-Esteem?

Simply explained, self-esteem refers to your view of value and worth. It "describes your level of confidence in your abilities and attributes" and when your self-esteem is good, your "overall quality of life" is improved too (Cherry, 2022). Low self-esteem means that you will be demotivated in different areas of your life, and this will eventually affect your mental health negatively. Our self-esteem depends on "our opinions and beliefs about ourselves," and these are aspects that are not so easy to change (Mind, 2022). It's molded by your thoughts, the relationships you have, and your various life experiences.

Breaking It Down

According to psychotherapist Dr. Joe Accardi (2022), good self-esteem is created through 10 important elements. If you are able to cultivate a few of these attributes, you will be a step closer to creating a foundation of optimism to nurture positive self-esteem that will remain with you throughout your life (Accardi, 2022):

- The first element is the feeling of **personal and interpersonal security**. Dr. Accardi says that a child needs to feel safe and secure in all ways that exist, such as in their "familial relationships, home environment, themselves, and their potential future."

- The second element is the sense of **social belonging**. You might already know how important this quality is, especially when it comes to your kids' friendships and acquaintances. Your child needs to feel secure and accepted in most of the social environments they are part of, such as friend groups in school, religious gatherings, extracurricular groups like school bands or sports teams, and even other family members. Children who are accepted and feel loved or valued by these groups usually have better self-esteem.

- The element of **trust** is the next important one and as mentioned at the beginning of the chapter, trust will help you conquer self-esteem issues. You need to be able to trust people but also have that feeling returned to you. As a parent, letting your child know that you trust them plays a massive role in getting them to trust themselves. The easiest way to do this is to make sure you give them the chance to discover this by giving them some responsibility that you know they are capable of handling safely. In this way, they will learn to trust themselves to complete the task and be independent. Of course, you need to remember to give them the space to finish the task without constantly checking up on them. For them to trust you, never go back on your word.

- Building on the sense of trust is the feeling of **being capable**. Accardi says that a child who's "encouraged to pursue her dreams and ambitions and allowed to independently tackle challenges she encounters along the way (with parental support when she requires it, of course), will see that she's competent." By ensuring that this condition is met, you will nurture a child who has the confidence to use problem-solving skills and also make decisions by themselves. It's also important that during this stage, you allow your child to make mistakes and attempt to rectify them by themselves.

- You'll find that having a **purpose** plays an important role in achieving proper happiness. Setting goals as a teen, and as a parent for your child, provides a sense of direction that gives you something to work toward and will fill you with satisfaction when achieved.

- Perhaps one of the most vital elements is the "feeling of **self-control**." Proper expectations in all environments, but especially at home, need to be created, and your child needs to have the opportunity to "meet those expectations independently." This creates an environment where your kid can comfortably nurture self-discipline and, ultimately, a sense of self-control.

- **Influence** is the element that is involved in feeling like you have an impact on your surroundings. Kids need to have the chance to feel like their opinions, ideas, and suggestions matter. This makes them feel like they're in charge of their own decisions. Accardi states that this gives them "a feeling of control over their environment."

- In addition to having a certain degree of influence in their environments, the **ability to contribute** to an overall outcome gives them a sense of importance. This is an aspect that can be nurtured and developed by parents and caregivers by allowing the child to have the opportunity to contribute to household events.

- The feeling of **reward** is not a new concept. Everyone craves being rewarded when they do something they believe is worth something. In the same way, even though your kid might have mastered the element of independence, they still need to be rewarded in some way. This doesn't always mean that you need to buy them something new, like fancy clothes or a new iPhone. Rewards can come in the form of gentle, kind, and approving acknowledgment from the parent or caregiver. It means making sure they know that you are proud of them and what they have achieved.

- **Family pride** can be a huge factor in uplifting your child's self-esteem. If they're proud of where they come from, and what their family has accomplished, they will find a positive sense of self-worth. It helps significantly when families are part of the activities and events that the child is involved in and this, in turn, boosts their self-esteem (Accardi, 2022).

These 10 components will empower your child and give them the chance to become independent and make decisions that boost their ability to problem-solve and gain a sense of control over the challenges they may face in their lives. They will develop a strong identity and will feel validated in their environment. By taking these elements into consideration when raising your kid, you will be able to help them cultivate a positive perception of themselves and lay the foundation for a strong and healthy self-esteem.

The Psychological Insights You Thought You Knew

Researchers at Washington University (McElroy, 2015) have discovered that even at the age of 5, kids can have self-esteem that is similar to what you would find in adults (McElroy, 2015). This means that by the time your child goes to kindergarten, they will already have developed a sense of self-esteem. Dario Cvencek, who is a scientist in research at the UW's Institute for Learning & Brain Sciences (I-LABS) says that their work "provides the earliest glimpse to date of how preschoolers sense their selves," and they have found that at the age of 5, "self-esteem is established strongly enough to be measured using sensitive techniques" (McElroy, 2015).

Their experiment involved having the kids listen to positive and negative words and respond with "me" or "not me" depending on how they felt about the words. The findings indicated that the kids identified more with the good words compared to the negative ones. The other tests performed were gender identity and preference tasks to determine if they understood their gender and what their preferred gender in other kids was. When these results were read in conjunction, it was determined that "self-esteem is not only unexpectedly strong in children this young but is also systematically related to other fundamental parts of children's personality, such as in-group preferences and gender identity" (McElroy, 2015).

The research that Cvencek and his team did reinforces how vital self-esteem is in the early stages of social development.

The Brain Game

When it comes to self-esteem, psychological constructs play an important role. They have the ability to shape our perceptions, relationships, and overall well-being. The brain and mind is a complicated place, and the connection between the mind and brain is an intricate one. Understanding the neuroscientific aspect can bring you a step closer to insights into how the inner brain, thoughts, and behaviors can influence our self-esteem and, as a result, our entire being.

In these past few years, we have learned a lot about self-esteem. However, all of these learnings have not shown us the way forward when we're stopped in our tracks by low self-esteem. We take out our frustrations on ourselves with loads of negative self-talk and internal criticism. Many times, our difficulties are not even our fault. It could be due to aging or even some kind of ailment.

Luckily for us, there have been incredible scientists like Paul Gilbert from the UK's Kingsway Hospital and Kristin Neff from the University of Texas who have found that if you're "self-compassionate, rather than self-critical, especially in rough times, is more likely to help us rebound and may lead to greater success and happiness in the long run" (Nixon, 2011). They have discovered that the brain has three emotional systems that have an "evolutionary purpose and mediating neurotransmitters" that communicate with each other and have an impact on self-esteem, self-compassion, and self-criticism (Nixon, 2011).

Drive System

The brain has something called a "drive system." This system uses a neurotransmitter called dopamine, which is produced in the brain. This hormone is often referred to as a feel-good hormone, as it is "involved in helping us feel pleasure as part of the brain's reward system" (Watson, 2021a). With the use of dopamine, the drive system pushes us toward the attainment of things that we need, helps us to form relationships and learn new things, and assists with the development of skills (Nixon, 2021).

Threat-Protection System

You have probably already heard about the fight-or-flight response, and the brain's threat-protection system is exactly this. This system uses a chemical called neuro-adrenaline which plays a huge role in our response during a situation where we may feel threatened. According to Gilbert in Pompa (2011), this system might also be linked to self-criticism, and it can either be the cause for self-criticism or it could be triggered by it. Either way, when we sense danger, it's time for the threat-protection system to shine.

Think of it like this: When our self-esteem is being compromised in any way, such as some type of setback in our lives, or running into someone we believe is better or superior to us, this system goes into protective mode to help us. To do this, we might start being a little too hard on ourselves. Negative self-talk might make an appearance and we might even start to judge or criticize the other person so that we can run away from our own faults and problems. Most people's brains use the first two systems, the drive and threat-protection systems, as a way to deal with things that might not always be the best thing. Thankfully, there is one more system available to us called the mammalian caregiving system.

Mammalian Caregiving System

This is a system that gives us the capability to become compassionate and encourages us to extend that capability in a way that will bring comfort to the drive and threat-protection systems. The mammalian caregiving system basically acts as the perfect companion, mum or dad, or friend that you need in troubling times by making use of two key aspects. The first one is oxytocin, which is often referred to as the "love hormone." This hormone has the ability to "help us bond with loved ones" and is typically created through activities like "touch, music, and exercise" (Watson, 2021a).

The second one is what Gilbert describes as "intrinsic opiates," and this refers to the body's natural opiates like endorphins and endogenous opioids. Together, oxytocin and intrinsic opiates become valuable when we are facing some kind of turmoil or feelings of despair. This allows the drive system to change into a system that will give it "a proverbial spanking or the system that will give it a hug" (Pompa, 2011). Research has shown that the more beneficial one is the hug.

Thinking Points

Answer the simple questions below to help you recap, remember, and apply the important information you were introduced to in this chapter.

1. What does self-esteem mean, and how can a solid foundation of self-esteem help you to navigate life's challenges?

2. Which of Joe Accardi's 10 elements for building good self-esteem do you think are most crucial for personal development, and why?

3. How does the concept of self-esteem apply to teenagers?

4. How might the three emotional systems in the brain (drive, threat-protection, and mammalian caregiving) influence your self-esteem and responses to any troubling issues you have?

5. How does being self-compassionate, especially during challenging times, contribute to success and happiness in the long run?

6. How can the insights from this chapter fit into your own life or the way you approach parenting and relationships?

Navigating self-esteem in teens can be a frustrating and difficult time, but now that you understand the psychology behind it and its impact on your child's life, you're a step closer to a happier and healthier life. It's important to cultivate the elements discussed in this chapter such as feelings of personal and interpersonal security, social belonging, trust, capability, a sense of purpose, self-control, influence, family pride, and a sense of reward.

It is also important to remember that the brain contributes in its own ways to help you deal with self-esteem issues like employing the various functions of the drive, threat-protection, and mammalian caregiving systems. However, these are not the only ways to deal with self-esteem issues. The next few chapters will discuss the seven-step journey to unparalleled self-esteem, which will be an exciting and rewarding journey for you and your child.

Part I:

Your Role

Step 1:

Mirror, Mirror—The Power of Self-Awarenes

Your visions will become clear only when you can look into your own heart. Who looks outside, dreams; who looks inside, awakes. –

C. G. Jung

Self-awareness is the first step in the seven-step roadmap that will foster self-esteem in teens. The roadmap will guide you through every step of the way and help you understand the importance of self-awareness, learn how to love yourself, discover strategies for self-acceptance and self-love, build emotional resilience, embrace uniqueness, and create healthy relationships.

The concept of self-awareness can feel flustering and overwhelming. Taking this journey to discover more about yourself can also be terrifying. But looking at it in comparison to what you will achieve once you reach the highest stage of self-awareness makes everything worth it. Self-awareness is a powerful tool, and this step is the foundation of your journey through self-esteem. In this chapter, you will be guided through the understanding of the critical relationship between self-awareness and self-esteem. You will discover the practical strategies that you will need to enhance your self-esteem through an increased level of self-awareness.

What Is Self-Awareness?

Shelley Duval and Robert Wickland, psychologists and authors of *A Theory of Objective Self-Awareness*, describe the concept as your capability to "focus on yourself and how your actions, thoughts, or emotions do or don't align with your internal standards" (Perry, 2022). Simply, it is a skill that allows you to reflect on your thoughts and emotions with an objective eye, and use the information you discover to adjust your behavior and thoughts appropriately. It means consciously diving into your mind to understand your feelings and motives. If this is done correctly, you will be able to achieve a new level of growth that will give you the means to reshape your life without feeling all the negativity that comes with change. This is not an easy feat to accomplish, but with the guidance and simple strategies this chapter offers, you will be a master of self-awareness in no time.

Exploring the Connection Between Self-Awareness and Self-Esteem

There's a pretty popular phrase by Aristotle that places the connection between self-awareness and self-esteem into a great perspective: "Knowing yourself is the beginning of wisdom." The idea behind this thought is that you need to really look at yourself to understand your reality. Only by doing this will you have the knowledge you need to make a difference. When you have this knowledge, you will have a "better grasp of reality" (Blaine, 2020). You probably already believe that you know everything about yourself, but we're all really chameleons that change who we are based on our environment and the people we're with at a particular moment in time.

How do we know which one of those personality constructs is really who we are? When we're around certain members of society, we can be polite and conforming, and around others, we can be rude and judgmental. Then, in other instances, we might be insightful and intelligent, and again, in front of others, we may seem like we're ignorant. Our existence seems to depend on everyone else but ourselves. Have we ever stopped to consider the essence of our being? Have we ever asked, or answered the question, "Who am I?"

Self-Concept

When we start delving into the idea of our self-concept, we will be able to answer that all-important question of "Who am I?" The idea of self-concept is to identify how we think about and evaluate ourselves (Blaine, 2022). To do this, we need to look at the parts of ourselves that we consider the most significant in the following areas: our roles, qualities, actions, and associations. We can arrange these aspects into many groups.

- When we look at our roles and associations, we can consider our social and family relationships: Do we play the role of a mother, father, sibling, friend, or partner? We can also look at our jobs. Are you a manager, teacher, lawyer, and so on?

- In the context of our qualities, we need to observe our physical appearance and whether we have any other attributes. Some examples of this would be the color of your hair and eyes, your weight or height, and whether you have any health issues or disabilities.

- When we consider our actions, we can observe aspects like how we react in certain situations. Are we quick to anger, do we get aggressive, or do we simply feel sad and hurt, or do we just ignore the entire situation? We can also observe our hobbies and spirituality. Do we paint, read, or sing? Do we pray, and do we have some kind of belief in a higher being, or not?

- Lastly, what are our intangible attributes and qualities? We need to discover if we have an honest and hardworking personality, or if it's the opposite. We can look at whether we have a happy-go-lucky persona or not. There are so many different types of attributes of this type.

It goes without saying that when we do this evaluation, we need to be very honest with ourselves, even if it means discovering something we do not like. It's okay to find out that we have negative qualities because this means we can now work on improving them.

Our self-concept can also change over time, and we can draw some qualities from other places such as the people we spend time with or the environment that surrounds us too. Our experiences also shape these attributes. Of course, the majority of these are most likely going to be developed early on in our childhoods, but it is important to remember that it is not a solid and immovable construct—it will change as a result of our situation or events in our lives (Blaine, 2022).

Creating Self-Awareness and Improving It

We've already learned that self-awareness means to acknowledge and perceive our emotions, values, attributes, skills, and other qualities. We know that we need to observe them from an objective point of view. But how exactly do we do this in the most effective way? Through self-reflection.

Self-reflection, according to Perry (2022), refers to taking some time and observing your thoughts, attitudes, motivations, and desires in the deepest way possible. You need to analyze your emotions and behaviors and then ask yourself, *Why do I feel and act this way?* It's an important tool to help you discover the positive aspects of your life so you can keep doing these things, while also allowing you to identify everything negative so you can eliminate it from your life. The following strategies will be your path to self-awareness through self-reflection.

Strategies to Practice Self-Reflection

- **Be in your own company:** This is your chance to spend time with yourself. Take some time to talk to yourself and have a good conversation—yes, do this out loud! Hearing what you are saying will encourage you to express your emotions in a way that's easy to understand. It makes you collect and organize your thoughts so you're not feeling overwhelmed and struggling to make heads or tails of your feelings. As you're doing this, don't forget to make sure you're inspecting your emotions without any personal attachment to them. When we do this, we have the opportunity to observe both the positive and negative feelings and emotions.

- **Question yourself:** This is an important step when it comes to self-reflection because by questioning yourself, you will discover a lot more details about your thoughts, emotions, and actions than if you had to just sit and think. With each question, you will find yourself opening up emotionally and learning new things about yourself. Some useful questions to ask yourself are questions like, *Am I doing something that makes me happy? What have I done today that improved my life?* or even questions like, *What can I do differently today than I did yesterday?*

  Questions like this give you the opportunity to think and reflect on events that happened, how you reacted, and whether this reaction is something that will contribute to your self-esteem in a negative or positive way. If it is negative, you are able to make changes and rectify your response in that particular situation if it arises again, and if it is positive, you can simply continue this kind of reaction and reinforce this behavior in future similar events. You need to always make sure that your questions are open-ended because closed-ended ones will give you one-word answers that will not have any depth or meaning. You will not be able to evaluate and come up with solutions based on a closed-ended answer (Perry, 2022).

- **Meditation:** This is a technique that you probably already heard of. It has been used as a healing tool in so many instances. People who suffer from mental health conditions often find that meditation helps them to calm anxiety and reduce depression. Similarly, it can also help with your self-esteem because it allows you to self-reflect. Meditation gives you the opportunity to create a deeper connection with your mind and body. Take at least 5 minutes from your day, find a place that has a relaxed setting with as few distractions as possible, and sit down in silence. The most important thing you need to do to meditate effectively is breathe.

  Your breathing needs to be focused, slow, and intentional so you can clear your mind and create a sense of calmness. You don't need to have a particular focus, and that's okay. The point of meditation is to see if there is anything bothering you on the surface. As you meditate, you will notice that your mind brings up certain issues. For example, you might notice things like you forgot to do some kind of work or that the trees look wonderful today. What you want to do is focus on which thoughts are present for just a moment, and which thoughts linger and present themselves repeatedly.

These are the areas that you would need to work on. This is something for you to take notice of and note down because physical attributes are one of the factors that will contribute to your self-esteem. You might notice that most of your thoughts are negative, so you need to address these issues and work on trying to have a more positive outlook on these situations. Either way, meditation is going to allow you to be calm, relax your mind, and bring up things that concern you, while also keeping you in a state of relaxation so that you don't become overwhelmed. Remember to write down the issues during your session so you can work on them at a later time (Perry, 2022).

- **Gratitude:** Practicing gratitude is a fantastic way to improve your mood and overall outlook on life. In an article by Paulina Galindo, she quotes a statement from Melody Beattie: "Gratitude turns what we have into enough, and more. It turns denial into acceptance, chaos into order, confusion into clarity [...] It makes sense of our past, brings peace for today, and creates a vision for tomorrow" (2021). I can think of no better way to explain the effect of gratitude on healing and improving self-acceptance and self-esteem.

Gratitude is a simple tool that requires so little to implement. It boosts your optimism, combats depression, and when done correctly, allows you to have stronger relationships. Communities improve, and on the whole, this makes the world a better place. Make a list of all the things that you have that make you happy, and take a few minutes every day to go through it. We shouldn't just feel grateful for what we have but also show gratitude toward others who have made even a small positive impact on our day (Galindo, 2021).

- **Journaling:** Although this method may seem simple, journaling can be quite comprehensive. Make sure you have a channel that is private to you so that you don't feel restricted in what thoughts and feelings you can write down. It doesn't have to be a physical book and paper, you can type on your computer, or even record yourself on your mobile device. Doing this will let you track your inner thoughts so you can process your feelings and your experiences outside the difficult or emotional setting that you were in. It lets you look at the situation from an objective mindset.

Not only can you track what you felt at a particular time and how you reacted to it, but you'll also have the opportunity to write down what you would, could, or have done differently in that situation, so that when it happens again, you know you've already got a strategy to implement. Journaling is going to let you keep your thoughts on record, and you can go back to them every couple of days to see if you've implemented the changes that you needed to make.

Journaling also lets you find patterns in your behavior, and this is crucial in understanding where this behavior is coming from and what fundamental aspect you need to change to either remove it if it's negative or enforce it if it's positive. Not only does journaling track your feelings, but it also lets you express yourself in a safe way. You can vent your frustrations, which allows you to feel calmer and a little bit more at ease in general. It can go a long way toward decreasing the amount of negativity that you hold in your body and mind toward yourself and other people.

Journaling 101

Journaling can be hard. You might have the intention to sit and write, but when you open the book, all you have is a blank page and a blank mind. Sometimes, there are way too many thoughts in your mind, and focusing on just one is almost impossible. However, journaling is an important part of your journey to self-awareness. So, here are a few tips, tricks, and prompts that will help you awaken your conscious thinking through journaling. These prompts will fall into a few categories to help you narrow your focus and gather your thoughts effectively. Simply answer at least one prompt per day and everything that you think about and feel that is related to the topic. Keep them as simple as possible so it's easy for you to reflect on them when you need to.

- **Relationships:**

    - Which of your current family relationships make you feel the happiest, and why?

    - Are you currently in a romantic relationship? Why or why not? Here, you can explain if the relationship makes you happy, and which part of it brings you joy. You can also expand on the things that you feel are negative about the relationship and why you think your relationship is in this space.

    - What is the most important aspect of a relationship for you and why? Some examples of this would be honesty, loyalty, a sense of humor, and so on.

    - What positive aspects do you feel you bring to a relationship, and how do you think this impacts your relationship?

    - What five lessons have you learned from any of your past relationships? This can be positive or negative.

- **Your career and professional life:**

    - Do you enjoy your job and does it fulfill you?

    - Would you want to be in the same job a few years from now? Why or why not?

    - What do you want to accomplish in your career? How can you get there?

- How do you feel about your relationship with your boss and coworkers?

    - Do you dread waking up for work every morning? Why or why not?

- **Emotions:**

    - What kind of thoughts or emotions do you have the most? Are they positive or negative?

    - Do you have any regrets in your life? What are they and what lesson did you learn from them?

    - How do you handle your negative emotions like guilt, anger, and sadness?

    - List five things that will immediately turn your good mood into a bad one. What do you normally do when this happens, and what can you do differently in the future?

    - How do you handle emotional or physical pain? Is there another way to deal with it?

    - What are you most afraid of? Why? What can you do to get over the fear?

Here are some prompts that should put you in a more positive mood every time you read them:

- What is your go-to activity when you are feeling down?

- List five everyday things that give you the most happiness.

- What does self-care mean to you?

- List 10 things that you are grateful for.

- Write a little love note to anything that brings you joy. This could be a place or even an object.

- What inspires you?

Are There Alternative Paths to Self-Awareness?

Besides self-reflection, there are other ways to develop your self-awareness. You can get feedback and find out what other people think of you. You can do this by asking your friends, family, and even work colleagues to share how they feel about you. They need to be as truthful as possible when they share their opinions about the kind of person you are and the skills that you have. This can be a difficult process because, sometimes, people don't want to make you feel bad, so they aren't completely honest. But, there are ways to gather information that is mostly accurate.

You can ask questions that don't require too much of an explanation and the best way to do this is by asking closed-ended questions, such as, "Am I a helpful person," to which they can answer with a yes or no. You definitely don't want to push people to give you feedback if they don't want to. Perhaps the trickiest part here is that you need to be very open-minded. You are not always going to receive positive feedback. In fact, some might be criticizing and make you feel angry or hurt, but you need to remember the reason that you're asking for this feedback is to improve yourself and work on the negative aspects of your character or personality so that you can improve holistically.

Trying to learn more and gaining empathy for other people will also help to improve your own self-awareness. You need to be able to put yourself in the situation of another person and understand their views and opinions. If you look at things like body language and expressions, and the way people react when you communicate with them, you will be able to judge how they feel about you and what their opinions are, which can be used as a tool to identify areas of concern in yourself.

Thinking Points

Answer the simple questions below to help you recap, remember, and apply the important information you were introduced to in this chapter.

1. What is self-awareness, and why is it considered the foundation of the journey to self-esteem?

2. This chapter explains that self-awareness involves reflecting on your thoughts and emotions objectively. How do you currently approach self-reflection, and do you find it challenging?

3. What are the strategies for practicing self-reflection, and which ones do you think will be the most effective for you? Why?

4. Considering the prompts for journaling provided in the chapter above, which category do you think has the most significant impact on your self-awareness and self-esteem, and why?

5. Feedback from others is mentioned as an alternative path to self-awareness. How would you handle criticism constructively?

6. How does gaining empathy for others contribute to self-awareness?

If you don't go through a self-awareness journey, you will remain in a cycle that hinders your productivity and sucks out the joy from your life. You will never realize why you're unhappy and nothing seems to fulfill you, and as a result, your self-esteem will keep dropping lower and lower until it severely impacts your mental health. It might sound like a difficult and confusing task, but when you break it down to the basics, all you need to do is simply question why you took a certain action in a particular situation.

Step 2:

Love Yourself As You Are

Beauty comes in all shapes and sizes. –Emme (In Vanessa, *Body Positive Quotes*)

The second of the seven-step roadmap for fostering self-esteem in teens is to learn to love yourself as you are. This step will help you to love your body image as it is, and you will find some techniques to promote a healthy body image. The guidance you will find in this chapter will help teenagers find a more positive view of their body image in the kind of world where society, social media, and peer pressure influence and negatively impact self-esteem and self-worth.

Understanding Body Image

Having a positive body image plays an important role when it comes to having good self-esteem. And if you don't already have a positive body image, then you're probably struggling with your self-esteem. The best way to develop the kind of body image you need for strong self-esteem is by first understanding what exactly body image is.

Learning to love yourself can be hard. What do you think about when you see your body in the mirror? Are you able to see any beauty, or do you only see its faults? What are your emotions like? Do you feel disgust, shame, or guilt? What about reliance, dignity, or gratefulness? This conversion that happens in your mind when you see your reflection, in the simplest way, is your body image.

In an article by Moira Lawler (2022), she describes the American Psychological Association's definition of body image as "the mental picture one forms of one's body as a whole, including its physical characteristics and one's attitudes toward these characteristics." It's your opinion and feelings about how your body looks. Sometimes, you might not have an opinion about how you look, but other times, you might be extremely harsh and negatively judge your physical appearance; when you look at your body, you might feel unworthy. If you have low self-esteem, chances are you don't have a healthy body image. So, how do you get there? What does it mean to have a healthy body image? (Lawler, 2022).

To have a healthy body image, you need to be able to feel comfortable in your skin, and the relationship between your mind and body needs to be a positive one. It doesn't matter how your body looks. You should be able to appreciate it and accept all of your qualities, whether they are good or bad. You shouldn't accept the standards of beauty that you see on social media or in magazines as the ultimate standard of beauty—your understanding of beauty needs to be bigger and should comprise a variety of shapes, colors, features, and sizes.

If your mental health is good, as well as your diet, it's likely that you have a positive body image. You should not feel like your body needs to look like another person's and feel bad about yourself when you find that it doesn't. You should never feel ashamed of your body or be uncomfortable with it, and you should have a realistic view of your body instead of a distorted one (Lawler, 2022).

What Does Body Image Have to Do With Self-Esteem?

You know by now that body image plays a critical role in self-esteem, but what exactly is its role? The way you view your body has a significant influence on your self-concept, which, in turn, affects your self-esteem. Simply explained, a good body image equals good self-esteem, and a poor body image will mean poor self-esteem. If you are unhappy about the way your body looks, for example, if you have acne, you might feel ashamed of yourself. This could impact your self-esteem in the sense that you will have low levels of confidence.

You might not want to go out in public, and you might want to hide yourself. You might look at yourself in the mirror, criticize yourself, and feel ugly or worthless. All of these things contribute to low self-esteem, which will negatively impact your mental health too. It is critical to develop a positive body image so that you can improve your self-worth, self-acceptance, and overall self-esteem.

Factors Affecting Body Image

There are so many different things that could possibly affect how you see yourself. These could be internal or external influences. In an article by Frew (2021), some of these factors are outlined. It is explained that in some cultures, if you are skinny, you will meet the typical standard of beauty. We have seen examples like this via broadcast media throughout time, such as in magazines, on TV, and now even on social media, where models are extremely thin and, sometimes, underweight. It isn't only women who have to adhere to these standards of beauty. Men are also affected, and the typical physical attributes that are preferred are when they are extremely muscular and fit.

Additionally, Frew (2021) explains that family also plays a significant role here. The way you are raised and the lessons you receive as a child will play a role in your personal views of your physical appearance. For example, if you come from a family who constantly comments on how fat you are or how thin you are, this becomes a part of your being, and you subconsciously hold this as a beauty standard you need to meet. When you're in your teens with a physical appearance that doesn't match this, it begins to affect your body image.

Furthermore, Frew (2021) identifies trauma and abuse as another factor that has an impact on your body image. Perhaps it is not something that you would see physically, but people who have been abused tend to feel unworthy and ashamed of their bodies. They sometimes find it difficult to accept how they look or even cannot physically look at their own body most of the time. This is not a process that's done purposely, and you might not even realize that this is how you feel about your body. Other factors like social media and puberty also play a big role in body image, and we'll discuss this further below.

Puberty and Body Image

During puberty, the body goes through a whole lot of physical changes and, as expected, these changes will affect how you see your body. Whatever your gender, these physical changes will have an impact on your thoughts and how you feel about yourself. But, before we go into this, it's important to remember that everyone is different, everyone goes through puberty at a different time, and the changes that occur in the body will also be different. Even though they might seem unusual, the changes that your body will go through are normal, and it's important to feel positive about them so that it doesn't negatively affect your self-esteem. Of course, if you are having some strange changes that seem to be affecting your health, be sure to consult a medical health professional.

As a girl going through puberty, you will experience a growth spurt. Some of the obvious changes to your body that you may notice are that you might be a little taller, or you might have put on a little more weight or even lost. Another change you might notice is that your breasts have started to form and pubic hair has also started to grow. These changes are likely going to make you feel very self-conscious and tend to affect how you see your body.

For example, you might not be developing breasts as quickly as other girls your age, and you might see this as something to worry about. You could start to feel like there is something wrong with you, or you might start having negative thoughts about yourself. It is important to try your best not to compare your body with others around you and remember that some girls might develop later on in puberty. Your body has its own clock, and it will do things at its own pace.

Puberty in boys is often identified by the "crack" in the voice. He will also start to see pubic hair, and the external genitals will develop. This is a significant factor in body image and self-esteem when it comes to boys. Boys do tend to compare the shapes and sizes of their genitals, and when it doesn't meet the typical standards that are laid out as a societal norm or in their peer groups, it starts to affect how they look at their body, and they might start to develop negative feelings toward themselves.

Boys will also have a growth spurt, and they could get much taller than they're used to and will probably feel a bit awkward in their bodies. They will also develop some facial hair, and the inability to grow this hair early on in puberty while other boys have already grown it out might be a difficult thing to go through. Other kids may mock or poke fun at you for not being able to grow facial hair, which will affect your body image. Again, it is so important to remember that everyone goes through puberty differently and will have different changes in their body, but it is important to love your body no matter what its shape or size is.

Social Media and Body Image

The impact of social media on your body image and, as a result, self-esteem, is significant and is the topic of many controversies. There has been constant debate on the effects it has on people, especially teens.

Lawler (2022) explains that social media plays a pivotal role in setting society's standards of physical perfection. She goes on to identify that beauty has become almost unattainable and unrealistic to the point where people change their appearances with makeup, surgery, and editing applications. It becomes difficult to remember what they originally looked like. Additionally, social media has created a shift from the deeper meaning of beauty to sexualizing and objectifying it. You will see thousands of images on your social media feeds that have been photoshopped and heavily edited to create the ultimate standard of beauty that ordinary people are unlikely to ever meet.

Being exposed to these images on a constant basis can cause you to judge yourself harshly, especially if your body is different from the images that are constantly being thrown in your face. Most of these images are not even natural or real, and users take hours out of the day to make sure that they are perfect before posting them. Holding yourself up to these impossible ideals and standards slowly chips away at any positive view you might have had of your body and turns it into an unhealthy obsession with trying to reach those standards.

Signs and Symptoms of Distorted Body Image

Now, more than ever, we are seeing a rise in people having a distorted body image. Sarah Canney is an author and running coach who has struggled with a distorted body image for 9 years. In an article on her blog, she explains what it means to have a distorted body image and shares her journey. Canney (2017) describes her distorted body image as something that she didn't even know was happening. She describes it as a very slow process that just starts with little things. She developed the eating disorder, anorexia, due to her poor body image.

The little things that she noticed only later on during the healing process, was that she developed negative feelings about her body such as a sense of shame, especially with her weight. She says that over time, it got worse and worse, and her image of herself became more distorted. It was so bad that she couldn't even see that she was becoming so incredibly thin that her bones were showing through her skin, her hair became extremely weak, and the color of her skin turned almost gray, but she still believed that she needed to lose more weight.

There are different ways to notice whether you have a distorted body image or not. Some of these factors are internal, while others are external that other people will be able to notice and you might not. Canney (2017) also discusses these aspects and explains them in a little more detail. So, here's how you can identify if you're experiencing symptoms of a distorted body image.

Internal Factors to Identify a Distorted Body Image

- **Criticizing your appearance:** If you find that you are critical of how you look, then you probably have a bit of a distorted body image. This means that every time you look at your reflection, you can see everything bad about your body, and you always feel that you need to change it in some way.

- **Shame:** This could refer to negative emotions that come from the way people treated you because of how you look. An example of this would be someone who constantly mocked you or made you feel bad if you were on the heavier side of the scale. Every time you look at your weight now, it could be triggering negative thoughts about your body.

- **A perfect appearance equals happiness:** You have the idea in your mind that the only time you can be happy is if your physical appearance meets whatever beauty standards you identify with, and it's unrealistic. If you place your value and happiness according to these unattainable standards, it's going to give you a distorted body image.

- **Spending way too much time fixated and working on your weight:** If you are spending most of your time in efforts contributing toward reducing your weight in some way, this means you have a distorted body image. Most of your time ends up being spent counting the calories in your meals, exercising for hours on end, preparing meals, researching the lowest possible calorie meals that you can have, and maybe even not eating at all.

External Factors to Identify Distorted Body Image

As a parent, it can be terrifying to think that your kid could be going through something so severe, and there's a possibility that you might not even know about it. But, there are signs and symptoms that will help you identify whether they are struggling with their body image, so you will be able to catch and treat it early. Stanborough (2020) explains that there are several ways to treat this that work properly, and will help you to live a happier life. Some of these options include therapy as well as other ways to improve your body image. These methods and strategies are described below:

- **Cognitive behavioral therapy:** This is a type of therapy that is used quite often when it comes to dealing with mental health conditions and illnesses. This involves using your thoughts and talking about issues to adjust the way you think in a way that will help you overcome whatever issues you might have. The key to effective cognitive behavioral therapy is to recognize patterns of thinking that might be damaging to you.

  Typically, a trained therapist will guide you through the process of identifying these patterns, and they will enable you to alter these manners of thinking in a way that will bring more positivity to you. The therapist will make use of a sense of relaxation that allows you to have some kind of stress relief as you go deeper into your thoughts and try to understand these patterns. Once these patterns are recognized, the therapist will work with you to change these thinking patterns internally so that what was once a negative thinking pattern becomes a positive one.

- **Psychotherapy:** This type of therapy is also one that is used for people who suffer from various mental health issues. It helps to reduce symptoms of mental health issues and can sometimes help to address the underlying issue so that you can fully heal. This type of therapy is also used to help with your body image. Stanborough (2020) explains that through the use of psychotherapy, you will discuss the issues that you face when it comes to your body image. You have the chance to identify triggers and how you feel about your body.

This could bring to the surface any childhood traumas that you might have which contribute to a negative body image. Doing this will allow you to heal more holistically. When you talk about issues that were experienced in your early life, you might discover thoughts that you didn't even know you had about your body. Psychotherapy is helpful because you have a safe place to communicate your emotions and actions that contribute to your negative body image. It can be done individually or in-group sessions, since some people might feel having the support of other people who are going through the same thing might help you to open up or be more comfortable.

- **Medication:** Stanborough (2020) found that in recent research, in the world of self-discovery, selective serotonin reuptake inhibitors, otherwise known as SSRIs, are worth exploring for people who are trying to navigate challenges in anxiety related to body image. SSRIs are a type of medication that is prescribed by doctors for people who struggle with anxiety disorders. Research has indicated that this type of medicine can offer support when you're trying to reshape your perspective of yourself. It's the type of tool that doesn't provide you with an immediate cure, but it helps you navigate the twists and turns of your thoughts.

If you use SSRIs together with cognitive behavioral therapy techniques, it creates a more effective way to transform the way you think. It's important to remember that this type of medication might not be the right fit for everyone, and there are dangers that you need to consider. Be sure to have an open conversation with your healthcare professional so that they can guide you and inform you of the possible concerns with this type of medication in order to make the best possible decision and get the most out of your path to well-being.

- **Exercise** Physical activity and exercise have been prescribed for a whole host of mental health issues. You can never go wrong with a healthy exercise session, especially when it comes to your body image. Engaging in physical fitness activities can be an incredibly powerful method in your search for mental well-being. Breaking a sweat during physical activity means your body releases endorphins, which are those magical feel-good chemicals you would have heard of before.

This chemical is a natural one that has the ability to fight the anxiety that is generally a side effect of a negative body image. However, researchers found a troubling effect of using physical therapy as a method to counteract negative body image. They found that could possibly add to the idea that you need to exercise in order to achieve the ideal body image, and this is not what a positive body image is about.

Although, you can use this method to your advantage by focusing on what your body can do rather than how your body looks. When it comes to physical activity, focus on how capable your body is instead of on your weight and any other factor contributing to the negativity. Focus on the fact that your body allows you to jump, run, and climb mountains because this is a wonderful accomplishment.

Creating a Positive Body Image

If you are able to cultivate a body image that is positive and healthy, it's definitely going to give you a better, confident, and more enjoyable life. You will feel like you have more energy and that you can do so much more with your life. Your mental health will be in a better place, paving the way for accomplishment and advances in your relationships, career, and even social life whether you're an adult or a teenager. So, how can you create a positive and healthy body image? Ulrich & Paulson (2021) suggest some very simple ways to create a positive body image:

- **Try a media detox:** Avoid spending too much time on social media or other forms of media so you can reset your mindset when it comes to your body image. This will help to reduce the pressure of the "perfect image" narrative the media forces on you.

- **Try to eat healthier:** Balanced meals and the right nutrition can help you change how you think about beauty. For your teen, having a conversation about food might help them feel more comfortable around it.

- **Get active:** Try to do new things that will help you get stronger. This will help you appreciate all the things your body can do.

- **Be positive:** Make some lists about everything that you feel is great about yourself.

- **The right friends:** Ensure that the people around are loving, caring, and body-positive people.

Thinking Points

Answer the simple questions below to help you recap, remember, and apply the important information you were introduced to in this chapter.

1. How can puberty affect your self-esteem, and how can you navigate this struggle?

2. In what ways does social media contribute to unrealistic beauty standards, and how can one minimize its negative impact on body image?

3. How do societal expectations and media influence the issue of distorted body image?

4. Which strategy for cultivating a positive body image stands out to you, and how can you incorporate it in your life?

5. What challenges can you face in changing your perspectives on body image and how can a supportive environment help?

6. How can open conversations about body image be encouraged, especially among teenagers?

It's so important to cultivate and explore how to improve self-esteem in teens, especially when it comes to body image because many times this is where it all begins. Society's pressures have a huge impact, and ensuring you're part of an environment that's supportive and understanding is crucial.

Step 3:

A Moment for You

Self-compassion is simply giving the same kindness to ourselves that we would give to others. –Christopher Germer (In V. C. Smith, *18 Quotes to Inspire*)

In the kind of world that celebrates achievements and resilience when we face difficulties, we often find ourselves trying to navigate the delicate balance between self-expectations and self-care. Christopher Germer's statement above about self-compassion is a kind of beacon that invites us to spread the warmth and understanding that we usually give toward others, toward ourselves.

This chapter will take you on a journey of exploration and will guide you through the incredible significance of being compassionate toward yourself. You will also be equipped with practical strategies that you can use in your daily life to strengthen your self-esteem. This chapter is going to teach you how to be kind to yourself, and we will unravel the layers of self-compassion through insightful strategies. By the end of this chapter, you will be able to nurture the most important relationship with the one person who deserves your true kindness and understanding the most—yourself.

Understanding Self-Compassion

For some people, self-compassion might be a difficult or unusual concept to understand. This is mostly because it has never applied to them, but it's so important in this journey toward positive self-esteem. Neff (2019) says that self-compassion is the same as extending the kindness and understanding we offer to others and ourselves. It involves looking at and understanding our own suffering, just as we would do for other people. We should be able to respond to suffering with warmth and care, instead of criticizing and being harsh when we fail or find something imperfect about ourselves.

Having self-compassion will encourage a gentle understanding of what it means to be human. Furthermore, Neff explains that this approach involves acknowledging the difficulties we face and extending a warm hand and some comfort to ourselves in these challenging moments. We need to be able to accept that any setbacks and even mistakes are an inherent part of a shared human experience. If we can embrace our imperfections and open our hearts to the reality of life and self-compassion, we can have a deeper connection with ourselves and the other people in our journey of life.

Elements of Self-Compassion

There are three elements that play an important role in the concept of self-compassion, and they work together to contribute positively toward our overall well-being. Neff (2019) breaks them down for us and explains their significance and relationship with self-compassion:

- **Self-kindness versus self-judgment:** Being kind to ourselves in times of difficulty and stress means we're being self-compassionate. That's what we should be trying to achieve. We need to be able to show ourselves understanding and gentleness when it feels like everything is against us. Unfortunately, we don't always get what we want and in a time like this, we begin to feel angry at ourselves, often being our own harsh critics. We need to be respectful in our self-talk, and be kind rather than judgmental and mean. Sometimes, we might not even realize how harsh we're being because it's become such a normal thing to do, but this is a highly contributing factor to self-doubt and overshadows any kindness we might have had toward ourselves.

- **Common humanity versus isolation:** Part of the human experience is that we all have things that make us imperfect, and sometimes we feel emotionally exposed. This means that life's challenges will have a negative effect on us, but, the most important thing to remember is that we have a shared human experience. We are all in this together, and things that affect one human are likely to affect another. We all feel pain and suffering. We all feel sadness. You are not alone.

If you are showing compassion towards someone, it doesn't mean you're just feeling sorry for them. Being compassionate means showing empathy. It means looking at somebody else's suffering, understanding it, and being aware of it to such an extent that it's as if you felt it yourself. Once you are able to become aware of this shared humanity, that's when you will truly understand that other people feel this way too, and you will no longer feel isolated. This is the reason this is such an important element; being able to see the suffering and frustrations of other people as something that is shared removes us from this isolation.

- **Mindfulness versus overidentification:** When it comes to self-compassion, mindfulness is a key element. It will be your helping hand in ensuring your negative emotions are well-balanced. The reason it needs to be so balanced is so you don't unnecessarily magnify your feelings, or on the opposite end, push them down so you don't feel them at all. Using this mindfulness, you will be able to put yourself in the shoes of others who are suffering, which also helps you to look at your own experiences from a different and more appreciative perspective.

You will also have the ability to inspect your thoughts objectively and remain nonjudgmental toward yourself. Remember that this only works if you also don't suppress your emotions. You should not be ignoring any of your feelings. Mindfulness isn't just a technique that you use once in your healing process. It needs to become your way of life, something that you are constantly practicing. Doing this allows you to always be in an emotional state to handle any of life's challenges.

The Power of Self-Compassion

You might be confused about what self-compassion has to do with self-esteem, but Roberts (2015) answers that question for us quite aptly. When you practice self-compassion, it has the potential to enhance your self-esteem, which ultimately has a positive contribution toward your mental well-being. If you are able to develop self-compassion correctly, it also instills more confidence in yourself and your actions. This usually has a positive impact when it comes to criticizing yourself, which means that you might not harshly criticize yourself as you normally do. It equips you with the skills to look at yourself with positivity and teaches you to resort to understanding and thoughtfulness in stressful or difficult situations.

Roberts (2015) is a trained psychotherapist and carries out many therapy sessions. In one of her group therapy sessions, she decided to bring up the idea of self-compassion to treat her patients, and she had excellent outcomes. She taught them how to be self-compassionate and introduced it in the simplest way possible so that participants could use it as part of their day-to-day lives. The idea here is that you need to change your thinking in small ways to make this easy to do on a daily basis. The people in her therapy groups reported that they felt less critical of themselves when things did not go according to their plans or when they had a particularly bad day. They also felt seen, heard, and felt their feelings being acknowledged. They said that they felt their overall happiness increase. This contributed to an increase in their self-esteem.

She says that one individual in her group tried to introduce self-care into her daily routines. Everyone's idea of self-care is different and for this particular individual, having a more balanced meal contributed to self-care. She set the goal of eating every morning without being self-critical. At the end of the little experiment, she explained that initially, it was almost impossible for her to stick to this routine of eating every day because she fell ill. But, she tried to persevere and, using the self-compassion she had learned, found that instead of being critical in a harsh way toward herself for getting sick and not eating, she just packed some snack bars in her handbag in case she felt like eating during the day. She didn't crumble due to her failure but instead, showed herself some understanding and didn't place a whole lot of blame on herself. This, of course, made the load of negative emotions toward herself lighter, and she felt happier.

Exploring the Effects of Self-Criticism

I'm just not good enough! I'm so stupid. Everyone hates me.

If you're struggling with self-criticism or have a kid who is facing this challenge, then these phrases are probably pretty common for you to say or hear. This is what we would call negative self-talk. In this section, we're going to embark on the journey of one of the most challenging aspects of adolescence or the teenage years.

Self-Criticism and Negative Self-Talk

Talking to yourself is completely normal. We all do it when we're experiencing different situations in life. For example, do you have a huge presentation coming up and, and are you really nervous? Well, that's when you want to say, *You got this!* Some people simply don't have that motivational feeling to tell themselves that it's going to be okay. Instead, they tell themselves, *Don't even try, you're just going to blow it.* Both of these feelings and reactions are normal because sometimes we say these things to just fit in with our friends, colleagues, or peers, and sometimes we just want to blow off some steam.

If you find your kid making statements like this occasionally, there's nothing to really worry about. If you're noticing that this happens constantly, then they're heading toward negative self-talk and self-criticism. "Negative self-talk is when your inner voice is excessively negative, sounding more like an inner critic" (Healthdirect Australia, 2019). What this means is that your inner voice will always be putting you down and demotivating you. You will feel doomed to fail before you can even begin a task.

Why Are Negative Self-Talk and Self-Criticism Dangerous?

One of the most damaging impacts of negative self-talk is its effect on mental health, especially in teenagers. Research has indicated that there are a whole host of mental health conditions that arise as a result of negative self-talk and criticism. Elizabeth Scott, an expert in stress management and emotional well-being explains these effects in one of her articles. Some of the effects she focuses on are depression, generalized anxiety disorder, post-traumatic stress disorder, psychosis, obsessive-compulsive disorder, and social anxiety disorder (Scott, 2022).

Furthermore, people who often self-criticize start to develop higher stress levels because they eventually create goals that are so unrealistic that they become impossible to reach. Scott also found that success is limited because it inhibits the ability to recognize opportunities and grab them at the right time. But these aren't the only effects of negative self-talk that Scott describes.

Your way of thinking is affected too because you will genuinely believe that all the negative things you're saying about yourself are true. You will never be satisfied with tasks you've completed because you will feel that it's never good enough—it needs to be perfect in a way that's practically unachievable. You're very likely to feel depressed, and eventually, you might find your relationships suffering.

These probably seem like consequences that are too difficult to handle, but don't give up. Many people face this and there is a way to pull yourself, or your kid, out of this rabbit hole of negative self-talk. It all starts with identifying why it began in the first place.

What Causes Negative Self-Talk?

There are many reasons for this, but some of the most common causes of negative self-talk and self-criticism are anxiety, depression, and a lack of self-confidence. The company you keep is also so important. If you spend most of your time with people who see the bad in everything, you're probably going to have a hard time seeing the positive side of things. Not taking some time out for yourself to get some much-needed self-care can also contribute to self-criticism.

Being isolated all the time and not asking for a helping hand when you need it could take you down this road too, just as neglecting your health and having unhealthy habits would. If you're experiencing issues in any of your relationships but do not make the time or effort to sort through these issues will contribute toward the self-criticism route (Olympia Benefits, 2021).

Breaking Free of Negative Self-Talk and Self-Criticism

In our daily thoughts, especially when we're struggling with our self-esteem, negativity will often take the lead and control how we feel and interact with ourselves and others. It is so important to change that narrative if you are intent on breaking free of low self-esteem. The great news is that there is a way to get rid of all this negative self-talk. You can remove yourself from the clutches of self-criticism and rise above the negative noise. It's time to embrace a better inner dialogue—one that will help you in your journey toward better self-esteem.

Reducing Negative Self-Talk

To change your negative inner dialogue and see a noticeable difference in your self-esteem, you first need to find a way to cut down on how much negativity you turn toward yourself. Healthdirect Australia (2019) suggests some of the following tips to help reduce negative self-talk:

- **Catch it in the act:** Try to identify and be conscious of the moments where you're being self-critical. Are you speaking to yourself in a way that's harmful? Would you say these things to another person? If you would not speak this way to someone else, afford yourself the same kindness and don't say it to yourself either.

- **Challenge yourself:** One of the most important questions you can ask yourself when being self-critical or negative is, *Is this true?* If your self-talk is negative and false, then it's time to stop saying it. Most of the time, we simply blow things out of proportion. You might say *I can never do anything right*, but that's totally wrong, isn't it? There are so many instances when you have done things right. If you remember this, then you'll remember that this negative self-talk is probably exaggerated, and it's time for it to go.

- **Place a limit on negativity:** This technique can go a long way in helping you to reduce negative self-talk, especially if you're someone who finds it difficult to move away from this. Using this technique means you don't have to quit cold turkey. You just need to allow yourself to be self-critical and negative for a certain amount of time—maybe a half hour, or less if you can.

  You can also limit yourself to what you're critical about. It helps to stay away from things like, *I'm so fat*, and rather criticize how much you eat, if overeating is a problem for you. For example, instead of the usual, *I look like a whale*, you can change it to "I eat too much." It can be hard to limit your negative, critical thoughts, but you can do this!

- **Stopping the thoughts:** This one is definitely easier said than done, but the aim of this technique is to immediately grab that negative thought and try to "squash" it or "throw it away."

Discovering Positive Self-Talk

Besides simply trying to reduce how much negative self-talk you're engaging in, there are other ways to improve your inner critic. If you implement the following strategies suggested by Scott (2023) in conjunction with the tips on reducing self-talk above, then you can create magic with your internal dialogue and completely change the way you see yourself. It will work wonders for your self-esteem.

- **Change your perspective:** This strategy involves trying to see things from an alternate point of view. You can jot them down in a journal or speak them out loud in the mirror. Then question yourself about its impact later in your life—will this particular negative thought matter when you're older?

- **Name it:** Assigning an actual name, "Silly Sally," for example, can help you change the way you talk to yourself. If you personify the negative self-talk, it becomes easy to view it as a person, or a "force outside yourself." When Silly Sally starts her monologue again, it will get easier to disagree with what she is saying, and it becomes less harmful to you. It can also help you to see that some of your thoughts aren't even true because you will have an outside view of it.

- **Turn it into something else:** Sometimes, it can be difficult to completely stop all negative self-talk, so it can be incredibly useful to change it into something else. Not only does this help make the transition from negativity into positivity easier, but it is also beneficial in the long term in the sense that it will contribute to an overall positive mindset. To do this, you will need to identify any negative self-talk as it is happening and alter it to either be neutral or positive. For example, you can change a thought like *I look disgusting*, to a neutral thought like, *I don't like the way I look*.

- To make this a positive thought, you would change it to focus on something you like about yourself like, *My hair looks great today*. It can be challenging to find something positive about yourself, especially as someone who struggles with self-esteem. However, if you recall the journaling prompts and if you followed this step in the earlier chapters, you might already have a list of things you like about yourself ready to go.

Thinking Points

Answer the simple questions below to help you recap, remember, and apply the important information you were introduced to in this chapter.

1. What is self-compassion, and what impact does it have on your well-being?

2. How do societal expectations or your own self-judgment influence your response to a challenging situation?

3. How does the concept of humanity reduce the feeling of isolation in times of difficulty? Have you ever experienced this?

4. What is the role of mindfulness in self-compassion, and how can it improve your ability to respond to negative emotions and thoughts?

5. What's the impact of negative self-talk and self-criticism on mental health, especially in the context of adolescence? How can you rectify this?

6. What are the strategies for reducing negative self-talk?

Learning to identify and understand your negative thoughts can be challenging, exhausting, and might take you a long time. You might not be able to make these changes immediately, but remember that these thoughts and feelings have been a part of who you are for a very long time, so don't become disheartened when you don't see immediate results. Practice your self-compassion, and be kind and patient toward yourself. Try to be consistent, and you will eventually see and feel positive outcomes.

Step 4:

Building Emotional Resilience

Resilience is knowing that you are the only one who has the power and the responsibility to pick yourself up. –Mary Holloway (In P. Morgan, *Dozens of Famous*)

You are now ready for Step 4 in the roadmap to strengthening your self-esteem. This is a very important step because it will be responsible for strengthening your resilience when you experience any challenges and will reinforce your emotional well-being. In this chapter, you will learn the art of bouncing back from the challenges of life. You will also be provided with the knowledge and tools you need to strengthen and maintain your positive feelings and emotions, as well as achieve your self-esteem goals.

What Is Emotional Resilience?

Emotional resilience, simply explained by The Children's Society (2021), is "your ability to respond to stressful or unexpected situations and crises." Emotional resilience is different for every individual. It all depends on how old you are, your mental health, and the various incidents that happened throughout your life. Having strong emotional resilience means that when a difficult or stressful event occurs, you will have the ability to change and adjust to deal with whatever is happening. Of course, some people will be more inherently stronger in their emotional resistance than others. But that's okay because it is possible to strengthen and improve how much emotional resilience you have.

Is Emotional Resilience Really Important?

People often don't take the concept of emotional resilience as seriously as they should, especially because it is intangible, but for your mental health and self-esteem, it's a really important ability or skill to have. The BetterHelp Editorial Team (2023) explains the significant role that good emotional resilience plays in our lives.

- **Stress:** When your body is affected due to extreme levels of stress, you can actually become sick, and it will manifest in the form of actual diseases in your body. Having good emotional resilience has the ability to prevent how much stress affects your body, and can prevent you from experiencing diseases like stomach or heart issues, a compromised immune system, and even blood pressure concerns.

- **Anxiety:** We know that anxiety plays a huge role in our mental health and self-esteem. What we don't realize is that people with good emotional resilience have the ability to deal with trauma that they might have experienced during their lives, and face challenging situations with a little more ease. They are also able to control their anxiety in a way that allows them to carry out other daily activities and focus on the present. With strong emotional resilience, it becomes easier to reduce our anxiety.

- **Depression:** Similar to anxiety, depression can be crippling. A strong emotional resilience will give you the ability to deal with this depression. Just like how we are able to reduce our anxiety through emotional resilience, depression can also be reduced. People with good emotional resilience can find ways to be positive and make changes to any negativity going on in their lives, which ultimately reduces depression.

- **Life span:** Research has indicated that those who have increased emotional resilience seem to live a longer life than those who don't. There was a study done where people classified as senior citizens found that their emotional resilience contributed to how lifespans were affected among various age groups (BetterHelp Editorial Team, 2023). This same research also indicated that when people had excellent emotional resilience, they were able to recognize and communicate their emotions well, and they had a great connection with each stage of their lives.

- **Reckless behavior:** If your emotional resistance is not strong enough, you are more likely to engage in high-risk behavior such as alcohol or drug abuse, eating disorders, or other activities that may put you or others in danger. These kinds of dangerous activities are most often used by people who don't have strong emotional resilience as a mechanism to deal with difficult situations.

- **Work or school:** It can be very stressful for a person to constantly be meeting deadlines and having to work every day. This is where emotional resilience comes in because it protects your mental health from these high levels of stress, and allows you to adapt according to these individual challenges in those environments. It also contributes to success in these fields, gives you better focus and positivity, and allows you to achieve your goals.

- **Learning:** As a person equipped with resilience, your scope for learning improves because you are not held back every time you fail. Emotional resilience will provide you with the ability to recognize the fear and confront that fear so you can become more open to trying different things.

- **Social connections and relationships:** When you struggle with self-esteem and have reduced emotional resilience, you tend to keep to yourself and be alone. This means that you won't have strong familial relationships or connections with the people you work with, your friends, or your community. Eventually, this will affect your mental health more severely. Having a strong emotional resilience allows you to communicate effectively with people in your life. It is especially useful with relationships that are romantic or with people that you spend a lot of time with, since it allows you to tackle conflict resolution in a way that feels safer and is more functional.

- **The ups and downs of life:** We all know that life is a roller-coaster, and in one moment, you're having the best time, while in the next you're hurtling toward despair. Everyone experiences this, and we will never know what each moment holds for us until it happens. But change is constant, and it can be good or bad. We need emotional resilience the most when that change is bad. Change can bring trauma and other difficulties. You might experience the death of a loved one or something terrible that might happen to you, but having resilience lets you cope, survive, get stronger, and live a better life.

What Does an Emotionally Resilient Person Look Like?

An emotionally resilient person would look different to everyone, but simply described, they can navigate life's challenges with grace and strength. This type of person will often have a positive outlook on life, and they exhibit a unique set of qualities that does not falter when they are faced with stressful situations. They will be the kind of person who is constantly experiencing personal growth, and their self-esteem is more than likely at a balanced stage. Let's take a look at some of the traits, as described by Waters (2013), of individuals who are emotionally resilient and thrive in life's unpredictable challenges.

- **Knowing their limits and boundaries:** Resilient individuals have the ability to differentiate between the kind of person that they are and the reason for their emotional disturbances. They also understand that their current difficult state is not going to be there forever. They do feel trauma, and they do feel stress, but it does not become a part of who they are, and they are able to rise above it.

- **Spending time with the right people:** It is often said that "you are the company you keep," and in the case of resilient individuals, this is especially true. These types of people keep friends and colleagues who have a similar kind of emotional resilience close to them. They don't spend time with people who are constantly negative. They spend time with these positive people in a friendship capacity, and they support each other when needed. This creates a network of friends or people who are dependable and have the ability to keep each other emotionally stable and reduce stress.

- **Self-awareness:** You might remember that self-awareness was one of the steps in the seven-step roadmap to improving self-esteem. People who are emotionally resilient nurture this ability of self-awareness. They're able to analyze their feelings, emotions, and actions, as well as understand what they require in an emotional sense and how to fix it. They can also recognize when things are too much for them and seek help when needed.

- **Acceptance:** Emotionally resilient people understand that sometimes, the challenges of life are inevitable and it can be emotionally draining. This type of person understands that things will sometimes be difficult to go through, and their traumas might last a long time or have a big impact on their mental health. But, they have the ability to accept that healing doesn't happen immediately. It takes patience and time. They don't fixate on what they can't control and place a lot of trust in themselves and their abilities.

- **Enjoy their own company:** Instead of finding ways to occupy themselves in a nonconstructive way such as binge-eating, engaging in high-risk behavior like drug and alcohol consumption, and spending time with toxic people in toxic environments, emotionally resilient people are able to sit by themselves and self-reflect or meditate. They have the capability to live in the present without mind-numbing distractions that add no value to their emotional health.

- **Self-care:** They have good habits that contribute to self-care. They also always ensure that they take time to rest and relax so that they can restore any mental capacity that has been depleted by stressful events that might have occurred.

- **Positivity and realism:** People with good emotional resilience have the ability to stay positive and always see things from different points of view. While they do have a positive outlook on life, they also understand the reality of situations. They also have the ability to look at a situation and analyze if anything can change for the better.

Developing an Emotionally Resilient Mindset

To be able to cultivate an emotionally resilient mindset, you need to have a mindset of growth. Wooll (2021) explains that those people who have a growth mindset "believe that skill and intelligence are something that people can develop." She further states that this type of person will "believe that while people have inherent qualities and traits, success comes from constant personal development." It's important to remember that having a growth mindset and having a positive mindset are not the same thing.

Just because you are constantly positive or have a positive outlook on life does not mean that you have a growth mindset. To have a growth mindset, you need to believe that you can constantly develop and learn new things through dedication and practice. Growth doesn't come from being naturally good at something. You need to upskill yourself and constantly be learning.

Growth vs. Fixed Mindset

Wooll (2021) also explains that the mindset falls into two categories: the growth mindset mentioned above as well as a fixed mindset. While people with a growth mindset believe that skills and knowledge are aspects that need to be cultivated and developed, people with a fixed mindset believe the opposite. They "believe that talent and intelligence is something that you either have or you don't" Wooll (2021). Furthermore, when it comes to these mindsets, people try to categorize themselves as having either a growth or fixed mindset, but this is not the reality. You don't have to have just one or the other. Many people have a combination of both.

When it comes to these types of mindsets, people differ in several ways. Wooll (2021) explains that people with a growth mindset tend to welcome things that challenge them, but those with a fixed mindset prefer not to engage in challenges. If you have a growth mindset, you will try harder when things don't go your way, while an individual with a fixed mindset would stop doing whatever task they're facing difficulty with. If you have a growth mindset, you will believe that your knowledge and abilities can be enhanced or improved, but having a fixed mindset means that you believe that you have this talent already and that learning more is not necessary.

Generally, people who have a growth mindset are encouraged to see the success of other people, while those with a fixed mindset feel intimidated. This type of person also generally feels that they have nothing left to learn, so they don't have the need or want to learn. Criticism is a driving factor for people with a growth mindset. They thrive on learning how they can improve, and those with a fixed mindset are not open to criticism at all.

The Importance of a Growth Mindset and How to Cultivate One

When it comes to taking care of your self-esteem or trying to improve it, having a growth mindset can be a critical factor. It is so important to cultivate this type of mindset so that you have the opportunity to learn and grow. If you have this type of mindset, you are more likely to have the ability to face life's challenges, and more importantly, learn from it in a way that improves your life. If you don't already have a growth mindset, that's okay because you can develop one by following this step-by-step guide.

A Step-By-Step Guide to Cultivating a Growth Mindset

It might be challenging to step out of your comfort zone, but if you want to improve your mental health and have more positive self-esteem, then cultivating a growth mindset is crucial. This simple guide will give you the insight you need to cultivate this mindset. Fran (2022) provides a great breakdown of the steps below.

1. **Identify your current mindset:** As described by Fran (2022), the first step in cultivating a growth mindset is to know what your

current mindset is. Are you the kind of person who has a growth mindset, or do you have a fixed mindset? If you don't know which one of these you have, then it will be difficult to find the direction you should move toward. In addition to identifying your current mindset, it's also important to understand the reason that you want to change. Why do you want to develop a growth mindset, and how will this change your life? This will give you direction and purpose.

2. **Identify your improvements:** In this step explained by Fran (2022), you need to look at how you have changed for the better. Observe aspects that were too challenging for you before and are much simpler now. The reasoning behind this is so that you can look at how you were able to make it easier. Once you're able to identify this, you will be able to apply this to other tasks or activities. People with a growth mindset constantly look at improvements in their lives and how they were achieved. This is ultimately what you should aim for.

3. **Review the success of others:** People with a growth mindset are naturally motivated by the success of other people, so one benefit of this step is that you will also become motivated. However, this step also has another important aspect to it. Observing the success of other people will allow you to analyze what they have done to reach their success, and you might learn tips that will help you develop your skills just like they have.

4. **Get some feedback:** This is a crucial step because it will give you an objective view of your progress. Talking to other people and listening to their opinions on how you approach or carry out a task can be very beneficial for you. It will allow you to have important information that will guide you toward your problem areas that need work. The idea here is not to get approval or rejection from other people. It is simply to see what they see, then adapt your methods to develop further.

5. **Learn how to use the word "yet":** Fran (2022) explains that the concept of "the power of yet" was introduced in a motivational TED Talk. The idea behind this concept is that you might have a fixed mindset about aspects that you don't excel at. Sometimes, it can be difficult to remove yourself from that space or frame of mind. However, using the term "yet" gives you the ability to overcome this. In other words, you are not "yet" good at that particular task. Cultivating a growth mindset is all about knowing that the things that you are not good at do not always have to be this way. They are simply things that you have not mastered "yet."

6. **Learn new things:** A big part of developing a growth mindset means trying to constantly grow. You need to attempt tasks that you haven't done before so that you can learn new skills. It has to be something that you don't already have a talent for. It can be something like learning to surf or swim, riding a bike, maybe even cooking, or learning a new language. Doing this will remove you from that comfort zone that inhibits your development, and open your mind to cultivating your abilities.

7. **Making mistakes:** Always remember that it's okay if you don't do something perfectly the first time you try it. Making mistakes allows you to learn. Understanding what you did wrong makes you think about how you can improve yourself and do better the next time. It is all part of a bigger process and teaches you how to be better in every way.

8. **Kindness:** Just as you would show kindness to other people, it is important to be kind to yourself. This means that when you fail, you don't self-criticize or make use of your negative self-talk. Be kind and show compassion for yourself when you make mistakes. It will motivate you to do better and can also help you to rectify a fixed mindset.

9. **Learn from others:** As with most activities and tasks, looking at examples from other people can be very beneficial. In this case, it is good to look at other people who have cultivated and developed a growth mindset in their lives. If you do this, you will be able to look at what they have done differently in their lives to achieve this outcome and see if these strategies can help you in your journey to cultivate a growth mindset.

   There are many examples like this to choose from such as Carol Dweck who is actually the person that is responsible for the concept of growth mindset, and other famous personalities with this mindset are Albert Einstein and Larry Page (Pradeepa, 2022). It is important to remember that you need to choose a personality that suits your needs personally to get the most out of this step.

10. **Goals:** The last step is to set realistic goals. Goals motivate you, challenge you, and guide you toward achieving what you need to achieve. This step is a little more complex and the way you set your goals will determine whether you reach them successfully or not. The next section will guide you through the process of setting the kind of goals that will complement a growth mindset.

Creating SMART Goals

You could be trying to achieve something for hours, months, or years, but not see any progress at all. This is because you haven't set your goals properly. But setting a goal doesn't just mean that you should write down what you want to achieve. Goals need to be SMART: specific, measurable, actionable, realistic, and time-bound. Herrity (2023) explains that "by using a series of five benchmarks that comprise the SMART method, you'll be able to create concise goals and action steps that will keep you on track." But, how do you create SMART goals? Herrity (2023) discusses this below.

S for Specific

To ensure that your goal is specific, it needs to be clearly defined. This means that it should be easy to understand what you hope to achieve. You can create such a goal through questions like what you want to achieve and what the impact of realizing the goal will be, as well as what steps you would need to take to achieve the goal.

An example of a specific goal would be: "I will have at least two meals a day, breakfast and dinner, instead of skipping most of my meals," or, "I will do at least fifteen minutes of cardio exercise every day for one month."

M for Measurable

Having a measurable goal means you will be able to observe your progress in achieving your goal. To create a measurable goal, you need to ensure that you are able to track any tasks or actions, as well as the amount of time needed to meet your goal.

For example, if you are struggling with an eating disorder and your goal is to eat more, a measurable goal in this instance would be: "By June, I will be eating breakfast every day, and this will include one glass of juice and at least one type of food classified as a carbohydrate." If you are looking at becoming fitter or stronger, a measurable goal will look like this: "By the end of January, I will increase my number of push-ups by twenty."

A for Achievable

Having an achievable goal means it is a type of goal that is attainable. It needs to be a goal that can actually be achieved and not one that's unrealistic. If you are a person who is trying to lose weight, for example, you cannot set a goal to lose 22 lb (10 kg) in 1 day. To create achievable goals, you can also develop new skills you might need. You can ask the relevant people questions that might help you toward achieving the goal.

A good example of an achievable goal would be to start exercising every day and eat a healthy and balanced meal daily. You can break this goal down further and add the measurable aspect to it and say, *I will exercise every day and eat a healthy and balanced meal so that by January I am at a healthy weight.* You can also add your goal weight here, provided it is not dangerously low.

R for Relevant

Relevant goals will allow you to get closer to what you want to achieve. Every step you take and decision you make should directly impact achieving your goal. It needs to be related to what you ultimately want to achieve. For example, if the outcome you want is to get healthier, your goal can't be to eat on time since this is not the action you need to take to achieve a healthy lifestyle.

An example of a relevant goal in this context would be: "I will eat healthy, balanced meals that have all of the nutrients needed for my body to become healthy, and I will also exercise regularly to stay active."

T for Time

Having a time-based or time-bound goal means that it is deadline-driven. Having goals within an appropriate deadline makes you more likely to achieve the goal. Of course, you need to look at a realistic deadline. You don't want to give yourself too short of a timespan to achieve something because when you don't achieve it within this period, you might become demotivated. An appropriate timeframe considers all of the above aspects when setting a goal. So, once you look at your goal's relevance, how specific it is, and whether it's achievable, you will be able to set a timeframe that will work for you.

Don't forget that everyone's goals are different, and it's important not to get discouraged when you feel that you are not on the same level as somebody else. Keep doing what you're doing, and you will achieve your goals, especially if they are SMART ones.

How to Turn Setbacks into Success

As a teenager or a parent of a teenager, it can be challenging when failures are experienced. Failures and difficulties can be disappointing and demotivating. It also comes with its fair share of emotional turmoil. So, how can you help your kid when they go through this? Here are a few important tips for turning setbacks into success, as explained by the MyTutor Blog for Parents (2023):

- **Listen to their feelings:** If your kid is opening up to you about some kind of setback that they have experienced, it's because they need support. They are already feeling angry, upset, and hurt. If your kid is already suffering from self-esteem issues, then they're probably already self-criticizing and thinking that they will never be "good enough." So, a great tip here is to listen to what they're telling you even if it's not the whole story. You don't need all the details to provide them with understanding and acknowledgment.

- **Promote acceptance of errors and failures:** Teenagers get embarrassed easily and when they experience setbacks, their concerns about this worsen. They don't want to look silly, especially in front of their friends. As a parent, you will have the opportunity to shape the way they feel about mistakes. This is the time when you need to help them understand that making mistakes is no big deal and that it allows them to learn how to be better. Show them that mistakes can be a good thing and that there is no need to be ashamed of them. It's a great idea to make use of real-life examples to demonstrate this idea to them. If you do this, they are more likely to believe you.

- **Help them work through it:** The next tip is to sit with them and help them understand why they made this mistake. It's very important not to approach this in a confrontational manner because they need to know that you are not angry or upset with them, but rather that you understand them, and that you were there to help them.

- **Show them all the positive learnings:** After the setback has occurred, it's always a good idea to look back at what happened during the failure and how it was fixed. Focus on all the positive aspects that came out of the setback. You can look at the new things that they learned and show them how the failure had a positive impact on their life. Doing this will help them realize that there is no need to fear failure.

Thinking Points

Answer the simple questions below to help you recap, remember, and apply the important information you were introduced to in this chapter.

1. What is emotional resilience, and why is it important for your self-esteem?

2. What are the key traits of an emotionally resilient person?

3. What does it mean to have a growth mindset, and how does having one benefit your personal development and self-esteem?

4. How can you cultivate a growth mindset?

5. Explain what it means to have a SMART goal, and why it is important.

Always remember that everyone has a different level of resilience, and you should not compare yourself to other people who are stronger in this aspect. Everyone has their own pace when it comes to developing and cultivating a stronger emotional resilience. So, take your time and work on building this aspect of your life using the following tips and techniques.

Step 5:

The Beauty of Self-Acceptance

Self-love is an ocean and your heart is a vessel. Make it full, and any excess will spill over into the lives of the people you hold dear. But you must come first. –Beau Taplin (In S. Zitz, *Get Inspired With These*)

We have heard people talking about self-love and self-acceptance all the time, but do we really understand what it means? In this chapter, we will dive deeply into the role of self-acceptance and its relationship to building healthy self-esteem. This chapter will be your guide to understanding self-acceptance, and you will learn all the critical insights, tips, and strategies that you will need to master this fifth step in the road map to better self-esteem.

What Is Self-Acceptance, and Why Does It Matter?

Self-acceptance can be a confusing concept, but simply explained, "it is the state of complete acceptance of oneself" (Kuttappa, 2022). Kuttappa further explains that being self-accepting means that regardless of how skilled, smart, or how you look, you embrace yourself and are happy with who you are. It is "an individual's acceptance of all of his/her attributes, positive or negative" (Kuttappa, 2022). Most times it is easy to accept all the positive things about ourselves, but having the quality of self-acceptance means that we need to accept all that is dark, gloomy, and bad too.

Why Is Self-Acceptance Important?

There are so many reasons that self-acceptance is a significant factor in self-esteem improvement, but perhaps the most important one is that "it is only by truly accepting ourselves that we can even begin the process of meaningful self-improvement." (Kuttappa, 2022). Life coach Perera (2020) describes the value of self-acceptance in one of his informative articles:

- **Self-acceptance gives you the ability to face challenges:** Finding the strength to meet any difficulty is incredibly hard, and one of the best ways to do this is by accepting who you truly are. Hiding the parts of yourself that you feel weak just makes it harder to face challenges, but when you begin to accept everything about yourself, especially the things that cannot change such as how you look, your personality, or your qualities, you will be able to improve your self-image and become stronger in your sense of self. This will help you to face life's challenges with a little more ease.

- **Prevents inner conflict:** If there is no self-acceptance, you open the door to a very negative impact on yourself. Your self-esteem will decrease drastically, and you might go about living a meaningless life—you end up becoming someone you're not. This just makes you feel unfulfilled, and you don't get any joy out of life. Once you don't accept yourself, you start to listen to what other people say about you and believe that negativity to be true. This can make you lose your sense of self and increase self-hatred.

- **Improves self-awareness:** Being able to fully accept yourself as you are means that you know everything positive and negative about yourself. When you have looked deep into yourself to achieve your self-acceptance, you will automatically become more self-aware. Being able to identify the good and the bad and be so self-accepting regardless, contributes to incredible self-awareness, which leads to overall happiness and better self-esteem.

- **Reduced self-criticism:** Truly looking at yourself, especially when it comes to things that you might not fully like about yourself, but still being able to find that acceptance has a big impact on reducing your self-criticism. When you can look at negative aspects of yourself such as a body weight that you are not happy with, skin tone you don't like, or your height, but you can still find happiness and be comfortable with who you are You will no longer speak to yourself in that harsh and uncompassionate way. This will do wonders for your self-esteem.

The Self-Esteem, Self-Love, and Self-Worth Equation

These three concepts have a very close relationship with each other. They all work together and form a powerful combination of elements that boost and improve your self-esteem. They become a solid foundation that you build your self-esteem upon. A lack of self-love reduces your self-worth, and low self-worth diminishes your self-esteem.

Self-worth can be defined as the "feeling that you are a good person who deserves to be treated with respect" (Ackerman, 2018). It forms the basis of who we believe we are. Ackerman (2018) explains that when we try to understand our self-worth, we look at aspects like our achievements and abilities and judge them. It could also be aspects like the way we look, who our friends are, our jobs, and our accomplishments in life. We use all of these factors to determine whether we are worthy people or not. If we feel our self-worth is high, then our self-love also increases.

On the other hand, low self-worth means our self-love will also decrease. This is because if we are unhappy with our appearance or other accomplishments in life, we start to feel that we have no value and that we aren't important enough. When this happens, we don't feel worthy of our own love. But this is so dangerous and damaging for our self-esteem because once you let go of self-love, you no longer feel good about yourself, and it impacts you negatively in every other aspect of your life. You will start to believe that if you can't love yourself, no one else can either.

Simply explained, self-esteem equals self-love plus self-worth. Overall, they all contribute to self-acceptance, which boosts self-confidence and makes you a happier, wholesome person who can be more content with your life.

Achieving Self-Acceptance

Now that you understand what self-acceptance is and the role that it plays in your self-esteem, let's look at the best way to achieve it. The journey to self-acceptance is a scary one because it means that you have to look at things about yourself that you otherwise would ignore. These things can be difficult to look at because they may have been born from trauma or some other difficulty in your life. These aspects might be the same things that are reducing your self-esteem, making you feel terrible about yourself, and causing self-hatred, but tackling these areas, bringing them to the surface, and coming to terms with them will be the best moment of your life.

Embracing Imperfections

This is probably the last thing you even want to look at. Nobody wants to look at everything that makes them imperfect. We do not want to look at our flaws because they are uncomfortable, and it can be very painful thinking about them. However, Dugan (2021), a practiced emotional and physical health therapist, found a few reasons why we should do exactly that.

- **It keeps you focused:** Keeping yourself away from being perfect all the time and embracing your imperfections will help you to stay focused on everything that matters. If you always want to achieve complete perfection, it becomes very easy to get distracted by all the small things that don't go according to plan. You fixate on details that don't matter in the grand scheme of things, and this prevents you from achieving the goals that you set out in the first place.

- **Improves your mood:** Being okay with your imperfections will allow you to reduce the amount of stress that you place on yourself. Self-criticism reduces drastically, and you will be happier because you will be living a stress-free life. Your mental load lightens and you will find yourself free to do the things that make you happy. You will be able to focus on growing and achieving a healthier and happier mindset and quality of life.

- **Being in the present:** Learning to accept yourself with all of your flaws just as you are helps you to become a person who focuses on your life as it is now. You'll be able to find enjoyment in the present moment because you won't be focused on constantly trying to achieve something years from now, or obsessing over things that happened a long time ago. You will be able to live in the present, cherish every moment, and be happy and satisfied with yourself and your life as it is now.

- **Improved compassion:** Self-acceptance helps you with your relationship with other people. Once you're able to be more patient, kind, and understanding toward yourself, you'll be able to extend this compassion to other people. Accepting your imperfections and being happy with yourself the way you are, allows you to also accept other people's imperfections, understand them, and show them more kindness.

- **Improved relationships:** Understanding that your imperfections make you who you are allows you to be a better person. It humbles you and teaches you that mistakes are okay and that everyone makes them. When this mindset is developed, you understand people better, and your relationships with the people that are around you become stronger.

- **A new perspective:** Embracing your imperfections will give you a new perspective on life. It teaches you to be part of a broader picture, and you become more aware of other people. You become stronger, more focused, and more determined. It opens up so many new possibilities and gives life a new meaning.

Embracing imperfections is scary and difficult, but once you get through it, you will love yourself more and appreciate everything unique about yourself. Here are some important tips and strategies to help you learn how to embrace your imperfections. These strategies will help you cultivate self-acceptance too!

Strategies for Cultivating Self-Acceptance

The first and most important step toward self-acceptance is being able to embrace your imperfections. McGinley (2017) explains some easy ways that you can learn to embrace everything imperfect about yourself:

1. **Imperfections in others:** One of the easiest ways to cut yourself some slack and embrace your imperfections is to look at other people's imperfections. The way you respond and view their imperfections or flaws allows you to be kinder to yourself. For example, if you know someone who is overweight, but you still like them and don't let their appearance bother you or change the way you view them as a person, you will be able to embrace your own weight if this is a concern for you. Learning to accept the imperfections in other people helps you to reduce your own self-criticism and accept yourself as you are.

2. **Imperfection and improvements of yourself:** You shouldn't take embracing your imperfections to the extreme. Do not accept yourself as you are to such an extent that you forget about trying to be a better person and trying to improve your health physically and mentally. The goal is not to achieve perfectionism but to achieve growth and be the best version of yourself. Embracing your imperfections means having a truthful conversation with yourself and finding anything that you can improve on, while also accepting that even though you have these flaws, you are still worthy of everything good.

3. **Your environment and circumstances:** Learn to accept that things aren't always going to be the way you want them to be. Stop trying to make everything perfect and don't stop doing things just because you feel like it's not the right time or not the right place. In other words, don't wait until everything is perfect for you to start doing what you want to do. For example, if you feel you need to do some journaling but don't have your notepad, there's no need to wait until you have it to get your thoughts down. You can simply take out your phone and type it out. If you

are constantly waiting for the perfect time to do everything, you won't get anything done or reach your goals.

4. **Love the process:** Ultimately, we should not be trying to achieve perfectionism. Challenges are what make life interesting. Apply the same concept to your flaws. Your flaws are what makes you an interesting person. Focus on trying to improve yourself, and learning about yourself, and take comfort and enjoyment from that process.

If you're a little confused about how to take these five strategies and put them together, McGinley (2017) explains it quite simply: First, become aware of who you are and all of your flaws. Meditate and when you do, take notice of your self-criticism and negative self-talk. Find out what is making you unhappy, then look at everything unique about yourself. The next part is the most important because this is where you will need to take action. The best thing to do is remove what's making you have negative emotions.

For example, if it's social media, then you don't need it anymore, or if it's friends who are constantly criticizing you in a way that makes you feel bad about yourself, stop hanging out with them. Take that first difficult action and everything else will become easy. Lastly, it's important to remember that as a human being, you are not perfect, you should just be "you." Your imperfections and flaws make you unique, interesting, and worthy.

Besides just embracing your imperfections, there are other ways to learn self-acceptance as well.

- **Own your uniqueness:** Your imperfections and qualities that you see as a flaw make you different. They make you special, so embrace these special qualities and let them make you stand out.

- **Turn your flaws into something positive**: Always look on the bright side of these imperfections that you have and try to find the reason that having this flaw would be a good thing. For example, if you are too detail-oriented, you can turn this into something positive by considering that being detail-oriented gives you the ability to carry out tasks that are well-researched and knowledgeable.

- **Be realistic**: Always remember that having goals is great, and they will help you to improve, but always make sure that these goals are not unrealistic. If you set goals that are almost impossible to achieve, you will stress more and your negative self-talk will come back.

- **Focus on how you feel**: Try to forget about how you look and place emphasis on your emotions and feelings. If something makes you feel good without looking good, then that's okay. Try to avoid stressing about meeting certain beauty standards or societal norms, and just do what makes you happy. For example, if yellow is not the color in season during Fashion Week, but that's the color that you feel you are most confident in, then wear that color everywhere you go.

Thinking Points

Answer the simple questions below to help you recap, remember, and apply the important information you were introduced to in this chapter.

1. Why is self-acceptance considered an important step in building healthy self-esteem?

2. How does a lack of self-acceptance affect your ability to face challenges? Will embracing your imperfections make a difference? How so?

3. How can self-acceptance contribute to reducing self-criticism?

4. What is the significance of self-worth in relation to self-love and self-esteem?

5. What are the strategies mentioned for cultivating self-acceptance?

The journey to self-acceptance is not an easy one. There will always be some type of barrier that makes it more challenging and, sometimes, almost impossible. We always want to fit into society, and this can be one of the main barriers that prevent us from trying to achieve self-acceptance. Social media dictates beauty standards and even financial status. Most times, this forces people to meet those expectations and try to fall in line with these norms (Saeed, 2023). We suppress who we really are and view our qualities as something to be embarrassed about instead of something to be proud of. We are also so terrified of being judged by other people that we start to shape and change our personalities so that people will like us more (Saeed, 2023).

Step 6:

Healthy Relationships at Work

Daring to set boundaries is about having the courage to love ourselves even when we risk disappointing others. –Brené Brown (In S. Martin, *16 Quotes to Inspire*)

Setting boundaries can be a difficult task. It isn't easy to tell someone when we've had enough because we always feel like we aren't allowed to express when we're not happy about something. However, boundaries are so important for a healthy mind and self-esteem, and as mentioned by Brené Brown in the quote above, when we set healthy boundaries, we are showing ourselves love and compassion.

In this chapter, we will dive into the power that healthy relationships at work has over our self-esteem. We will learn how these connections impact our well-being, and we'll discover practical guidance that you can implement to create and maintain these relationships in a way that will contribute to healthy self-esteem.

Understanding How Relationships Affect Self-Esteem

There have been tons of research and studies on how relationships affect self-esteem, and the conclusions of all of them indicate that the kind of relationships you have with the people around you plays a significant role in whether you will have positive or negative self-esteem.

In one study, it was discovered "that positive social relationships, social support, and social acceptance help shape the development of self-esteem in people over time across ages 4 to 76." (Indo Asian News Service, 2019). This means that the quality of our relationships has a direct impact on our mental health and self-esteem. It goes the other way too—a poor relationship with a lot of difficulties and problems will hurt your self-esteem.

Identifying Healthy Relationships

You can either have a healthy relationship or an unhealthy one with the people around you. Relationships are different for everyone. The kind of relationship that you have with your family will be different from the kind of relationship you will have with a friend, but either way, if you want healthy self-esteem, you need to cultivate healthy relationships. But what is a healthy relationship, and how can you ensure that your relationships with people contribute positively to your self-esteem? Raypole (2019) outlines some important aspects that all healthy relationships should consist of below:

- **Communication:** When it comes to relationships, romantic, familial, or even friendship, it is vital that you are able to talk openly and comfortably about anything that concerns you. You should be able to share issues that stress you out, such as difficulties at your job, financial issues, and even your emotional and mental health state. But more than you being able to talk to them, they should be able to talk to you too. You should be able to listen without being judgmental in the same way that they would listen to you.

- **Trust:** This is another key factor that is important for healthy relationships. Regardless of whether the relationship is romantic or not, you need to be able to be honest and not hide things from the other party. It also means that you trust in their character and loyalty. Of course, in return, you also need to be honest and loyal to them.

- **Being yourself:** Just because you have a relationship with another person doesn't mean that you have to change your entire personality. When your relationship is healthy, both parties can be who they are and have their own sense of self. You can lean on each other for support but not be completely dependent on them to function.

- **Alone time:** As important as it is to spend quality time with your partner, family member, or friend, it's just as important to spend time by yourself. Make sure you are prioritizing personal time and doing things that you enjoy by yourself. This could prevent feelings of suffocation in the relationship.

- **Intimacy:** If you are in a romantic relationship, physical intimacy will be an important aspect. Remember that physical intimacy needs to be comfortable for both parties. A healthy physical relationship means that both of you will be comfortable with each other. You should be able to talk about what makes you comfortable and uncomfortable, freely and safely. Intimacy in friendship and familial relationships is also important. Hugs and cuddles make a person feel safe and warm. Of course, some people are uncomfortable with intimacy of any kind and this needs to be respected in relationships too.

- **Being a team:** When you are in a healthy relationship, you will be able to work together even when you don't agree. You should be able to support each other to achieve your goals, even if you want something different.

- **Keep it breezy:** Life can be challenging, stressful, and traumatic. You need to have a relationship that allows some lightheartedness in these troubling times. Always make sure that the person you're spending your time with knows how to be spontaneous, and crack a joke or two. This will go a long way in reducing the stress that builds up and weighs you down.

- **Conflict:** All relationships have conflict and this is very normal, but the way you resolve conflict needs to be healthy. Any disagreements need to be talked about in a calm and collected way, without being mean to each other or assigning blame. You should be able to resolve conflict and feel as though you are heard even when the other person is disagreeing with you.

Recognizing Unhealthy Relationships

Relationships take work and not all of them will be healthy from the beginning. Sometimes, you might be in a relationship for so long that you can no longer recognize the signs that make it an unhealthy one. There are many things to look out for when it comes to unhealthy relationships.

Sometimes, one person becomes very controlling in the relationship, and this is not what an ideal relationship should be like. The person that you are with should never try to change who you are or try to control what you feel and how you express it. Another important aspect to look out for is how they respond to your boundaries. If your partner is not respecting any boundaries that you have laid out, your relationship is in danger of becoming unhealthy. Your partner should not be pushing you to do things that make you uncomfortable or try to manipulate you into doing what they want. This is especially important when it comes to intimacy, whether it's physical or emotional, and when you are asking for time or space away from them.

If you are not spending enough time together, your relationship will suffer. When you start to place importance on work or other events in your life, your relationship could start to deteriorate, leading to an unhealthy relationship. The way you speak to each other is also a determining factor in the health of the relationship. If one person is constantly rudely speaking to the other and being disrespectful, then this is not a relationship you should be in.

Negativity like this in a relationship is just going to keep you in a stressful emotional state all the time, and you are probably going to feel bad about yourself constantly. Ultimately, this will have a detrimental effect on your self-esteem and mental health. Relationships are meant to make you feel heard, supported, loved, happy, and safe—all aspects that improve your self-confidence, self-love, and self-esteem.

The Role of Communication

A relationship without communication will get nowhere. Misunderstandings are bound to happen and will ruin the relationship. If you want a healthy relationship, then good communication that ensures conflict resolution is effective will be of utmost importance. The Better Health Channel (n.d.) describes communication as "the transfer of information from one place to another" and in the context of relationships, "communication allows you to explain to someone else what you are experiencing and what your needs are." This allows you and your partner to help each other meet all-important wants and needs.

However, communication can be really tricky because more often than not, we expect people to just understand our needs and wants without us explaining them to them. It's important to remember that we always need to talk. We should always communicate clearly so that any unnecessary negative feelings and misunderstandings can be avoided.

Effective Communication Strategies

Here are some tips outlined by the Better Health Channel (n.d.) to help you with clear communication. These strategies should be implemented in your relationships with parents, siblings, partners, and even work colleagues and friends for effective communication.

It's important to remember that all people are different, and the way one person communicates will be different from another. Try to find the best way to communicate in your relationship that suits that particular relationship. Remember that communication with your mum and dad will not be the same as communication with your partner.

- **Put all the screens away:** When you are trying to have a conversation with a person, always ensure that you try to pay attention completely without being distracted by any outside influences such as your cell phone or laptop.

- **Be thoughtful:** When you are communicating, it's important to take the time to carefully consider your words. Try to be tactful and communicate what you need to say without being hurtful or mean. Think before you speak.

- **Be clear:** Always be as clear as possible. You don't want people to misunderstand and misinterpret you. Your partner needs to clearly hear exactly what you are saying so that they can understand what you want to tell them. If your words are not concise and clear, you are giving them the opportunity to interpret what you're saying in some other way and that might not be what you mean at all. This will cause unnecessary arguments and may lead to you feeling like you aren't being heard.

- **Relevant content:** During your conversation, you need to discuss what the actual issue is and the impact it has on you and your emotions. Try to make sure that you're staying on that particular point and that you aren't discussing things that have nothing to do with the conversation at hand.

- **It's about you:** When it's your turn to speak, talk about everything that you are feeling. Try not to assume what the other person is thinking or feeling. Your entire dialogue should consist of words like, "I feel that," or, "I want this." This helps you to clearly convey your point of view and also prevents you from slipping into a communication that makes the other person feel attacked.

- **Taking responsibility:** Remember that as important as it is for the other person to take responsibility and own up to any mistakes that they might have made, it is just as important for you to do the same. Conversations go two ways, and it will not be effective if you are unable to accept responsibility for the way you feel and the actions that you took.

- **Listening:** Everybody wants to feel heard, and so does your partner. When you are having a conversation, and it's time for your partner to discuss their feelings, make sure that you are listening and understanding them with an open mind and heart. You need to have empathy and sympathy so that their feelings are being acknowledged too.

- **Positivity:** Conversations shouldn't only be about everything that's going wrong in your relationship. If you've noticed something that your partner is doing well and something that they've done that makes you feel happy, make sure to acknowledge these too. It will make them feel like you don't only see the bad things about them. They will feel more appreciated and will be more open to communication and conflict resolution.

One of the most important things to remember during communication is that one person doesn't always have to be right or wrong. It is possible to love someone and have a healthy relationship with them but still disagree on certain matters. Always remember to understand when you have reached that limit and that it's okay to disagree.

Nonverbal communication is important too, and this is often overlooked, which makes one party feel like they aren't worthy or being cared for enough. When you communicate, pay attention to body language and the tone of your voice. It has a huge impact on how emotions and feelings are received. If you are trying to convey comfort to your partner, but your arms are crossed, and you are turning away from them, they aren't going to feel like you're paying attention or that you even love them. This means that they will not be comforted by what you are saying. Always make sure that your body language and words are in harmony.

Conflict Resolution

Conflict resolution is challenging, especially because most times, when you are arguing, emotions run high, and it becomes difficult to see things from the other person's point of view or to listen calmly. According to Amaresan (2019), conflict resolution is when "two or more parties work toward a solution to a problem or dispute. The parties involved work together in a productive way to achieve a result that satisfies everyone involved." For a healthy relationship with the people you love and even in a workplace setting, conflict resolution is a critical skill. Amaresan (2019) points out the key aspects of conflict resolution below.

- **Listening:** This doesn't just mean hearing what the other person is saying. When you listen during conflict resolution, it needs to be active listening. This means that you should avoid trying to respond as they're speaking and focus instead on what they are saying so that you can fully understand it. You need to have a receptive mind and ask questions if you need to clarify anything.

- **Being aware in an emotional capacity:** You might have heard the term "EQ" before, which you've probably associated with "IQ," short for "intelligence quotient." When it comes to relationships and conflict resolution, it's critical to have high EQ, short for emotional intelligence. Having high emotional intelligence will assist you in understanding your partner's emotional state, which is helpful in volatile situations. When people are angry, hurt, or exasperated, the situation can very easily explode. However, someone with a high EQ will be able to foresee the emotions that build up to make a situation worse and can take the appropriate measures to cool things down.

- **Tolerance and composure:** The ability to be patient is an important one during conflict resolution. You need to be able to be calm and persevere during your conversation. Many times, conflict resolution can take a while for a satisfactory conclusion to be reached. To reach your conflict resolution goals, you need to make sure that you spend as much time as it takes so that all emotions are heard and validated, and all possible solutions are considered.

- **Objectivity:** Whenever we get into an argument, it's not uncommon to bring up mistakes and issues from the past. However, allowing yourself to do this during a conflict resolution session will only make things worse and the problem you are trying to deal with presently will not be solved. To ensure this doesn't happen, you need to try to stay objective and impartial, only focusing on the current objective. Don't look into your partner's faults or previous problems. Simply focus on the current problem and solutions that will help solve that specific conflict.

- **Be positive:** When you're having an argument, it can be difficult to see any positivity in anything. You can become demotivated and feel like the problem is unsolvable, but it's important to put a positive spin on things. Finding a solution is going to be next to impossible if you can't be positive about it. If your attitude is positive, it will also help the other person—your partner—feel more comfortable, at ease, and open to solutions that you suggest.

- **Honest and open communication:** Dealing with difficult conversations and conflict can really take a toll on your relationship, even if a solution has been reached. Don't forget to always be honest, and leave an open line of communication. This will give you and your partner the opportunity to chat and see how you're both doing after the issue is resolved. It can sometimes take a lot of work to mend your relationship, and having access to open communication is critical.

Setting and Maintaining Boundaries

When it comes to maintaining and preserving your self-worth and self-esteem, boundaries play a significant role. Not only is setting proper boundaries important, but actually asserting and maintaining them will be a vital factor too.

Why are boundaries important, you ask?

Let's start with what exactly we mean when we use the term "boundaries." According to Moore (2022), the idea of a boundary refers to "a rule or limit you set with another person to express what you deem acceptable and unacceptable." This means that you will lay out your likes and dislikes, or wants and needs in a decisive and confident manner without conveying any negative feelings.

There are different types of boundaries too. Rainne (2020) explains them as follows:

- **Physical boundaries** are any type of boundary that involves your body or your environment. This would include boundaries related to people touching your body, physical affection, and even when you choose to interact with people.

- **Emotional boundaries**, on the other hand, involve your feelings. With these boundaries, you are restricting anything that affects your mental well-being. This means that you decide when you feel you are emotionally ready to communicate with someone after you've been in an argument. You get to choose what kind of conversations you want to have. If a topic makes you feel uncomfortable, you can choose to let the other person know that this is not something you want to talk about.

  You can also set boundaries for whether you are available to help someone else who might be going through a tough time. If you feel that you are not emotionally ready or that you're not in a safe place with your mental health, you do not need to give all of your emotional capacity and support to that person until you are ready.

- **Material boundaries** are those boundaries that refer to your belongings. This will also include your finances. When it comes to these boundaries, it means that you can choose when to allow people to use your possessions or borrow money from you if they need it. For example, if you aren't financially comfortable right now, and your best friend needs money urgently, you are not obligated to lend to them.

- **Time boundaries** are important because they limit the time that you want to spend in different scenarios, whether it means how much time you are spending with someone or how much time you are spending in your work environment. When you don't manage your time properly, you can very easily burn out, which is why setting your time boundaries is important.

  If you feel like you need personal time to work through some issues that are affecting you negatively, and you need to reduce the amount of time that you are talking to your friend to ensure you spend a sufficient amount of time gathering your thoughts, that boundary needs to be set. It also means being able to say no if you don't have the time capacity to take on additional work.

- **Sexual boundaries** play a huge role in relationships. Being able to speak about what you're comfortable with when it comes to intimacy with your partner can be a defining moment in the success of a relationship. You should be able to say no to any type of intimacy if you are not comfortable with it, even if it is just a hug or a simple kiss on the cheek. Your partner should respect your sexual boundaries always, and remember that this goes both ways. You should also ensure that you are respecting your partner's boundaries and that you always have mutual consent.

Boundaries are important for many reasons. Firstly, since they need to come from a place of assertiveness, they help you to ensure that people don't take advantage of you (Moore, 2022). They are also very beneficial for the prevention of burnout. Moore (2022) demonstrates that if you cannot set a boundary in your work or job, you will eventually use your much-needed personal time to carry out work activities at home. This can exhaust you and contribute to anxiety and stress. Having healthy boundaries can assist you in creating and taking care of your relationships (Moore, 2022).

Setting healthy boundaries in relationships means knowing when to have your alone time and when to spend time with the other person in the relationship. This applies to relationships with your family, partners, and even friends. It can also be helpful when you need to communicate what you're comfortable or not comfortable with. For example, if you don't like too much physical contact with your friends, then that's an important boundary for you to set. Andrade (2021) outlines a few other important benefits too, such as having the chance to improve your self-respect by setting boundaries. Furthermore, you're able to limit arguments and fights that could have occurred due to a lack of healthy boundaries in the future.

How to Assert Your Boundaries

Setting boundaries can be difficult. Sometimes, it's challenging to tell someone what they can and cannot do, even if it's related to your well-being. You might feel embarrassed or a little ashamed to set your boundaries, and that's okay. It might take some time to perfect it, but here are some tips you can use to set yourself some healthy boundaries that will help you improve your mental health, self-worth, and self-esteem. Nash (2018), who has a PhD in psychotherapy, outlines these important strategies below:

- The first step to creating the boundaries you need is to be self-aware so you know what you're looking for. Using the techniques you learned in the chapter on self-awareness, you will be able to identify what is good and harmful for your mental health and self-esteem.

- The second step is to ensure that you've brushed up on your communication skills. Tips and tricks to improve your communication skills were addressed above, and you can use those strategies to make sure you will be concise, clear, and authoritative when it comes to communicating your boundaries.

- The third step is to be assertive. This does not mean that you should be rude or aggressive when making your boundaries known. You should be conveying your boundaries in a way that considers other people's feelings so that you do not hurt them or make them feel uncomfortable. However, at the same time, you need to be authoritative.

To put this into perspective, all you need to do is know what your boundary is and then communicate this in a very clear way without being disrespectful. Tell the person your boundary in a positive way, speaking more about what is comfortable for you rather than what isn't comfortable. Finally, remember that you might have some negative feelings after setting this boundary. This is normal, and you will eventually get through it.

Empathy and Understanding in a Relationship

Most times, people forget that empathy plays a significant role in maintaining relationships. The reason why it's such a critical factor is because empathy gives you the opportunity to put yourself in the other person's shoes and feel what they are feeling. This helps you to respond better in various situations.

Nurhawa (2023) describes a few reasons why we should try to improve our empathy in our relationships. Firstly, it improves your personal relationships. If we are able to be empathetic, our relationships will have a stronger foundation. We will cultivate support and have better communication. Empathy will allow you to be more open to listening to the other person in the relationship and be more understanding when they express their feelings and emotions. It also helps you to improve your work relationships.

Empathy also helps with relationships that are outside of a personal setting. It will give you the ability to easily fit in with teams at work and will improve collaboration with your colleagues. Ultimately, it will improve productivity and make you happier at work. In a managerial position, you will be able to strengthen your team by understanding their needs and wants so you can support them where they need it.

How Can You Become More Empathetic?

Although learning how to be more empathetic might seem like a daunting task, there are a few simple techniques explained by Carpenter (2020):

- **Learn to listen:** Understanding things from another person's point of view begins with listening actively. When it comes to empathy, body language is extremely important. This will allow you to pay attention to the way the other person moves or holds their body. Most times, the language in their body reflects what they are feeling on the inside, and this will allow you to adjust the conversation or feelings accordingly. If you truly listen to another person with an open mind, you will be able to connect with their emotions.

- **Sharing feelings:** The easiest way to understand this point is to imagine yourself in another person's shoes. Once you feel as if it is you in that situation and not the other person, you will be able to feel what they are feeling. This allows you to truly understand the emotions and lightens the burden of the other person since you are sharing their difficult emotions too.

- **Being vulnerable:** When you open yourself up to sharing your difficult emotions with other people, they begin to feel empathy for you too. But it doesn't only need to be negative emotions. You can also project happiness and satisfaction. Either way, allowing yourself to be vulnerable will improve your empathic ability toward other people.

- **Speak to others:** To develop your empathy, you need to interact with as many people as you can. Try to take some time out of your day to have some conversations and chat with the people around you. Don't forget to be focused and listen to what they are saying so that you can notice their feelings too.

- **Body language:** When it comes to empathy, body language is extremely important. If you pay attention to the way the other person moves or holds their body, you will notice that the language of their body reflects what they are feeling on the inside, and this will allow you to adjust the conversation or feelings accordingly.

- **Remember to act:** Empathy doesn't stop at just feeling what another person is feeling. You also need to adjust your behavior or take some measures to help the person and offer them comfort.

Thinking Points

Answer the simple questions below to help you recap, remember, and apply the important information you were introduced to in this chapter.

1. How do clear boundaries contribute to your well-being?

2. What are the different types of boundaries that you should be using?

3. What is conflict resolution, and when does it apply to your life?

4. What are some conflict resolution techniques?

5. Discuss the role of empathy in your relationships, and how you can cultivate more empathy in your relationships.

Step 7:

Standing Your Ground

To be yourself in a world that is constantly trying to make you something else is the greatest accomplishment –Ralph Waldo Emerson

The final step in the seven-step roadmap to fostering healthy self-esteem is learning to stand your ground. It's so important to teach our teens to stand their ground, and this chapter will do exactly that. You will learn the vital skills and techniques to help you resist and overcome external pressures, including peer pressure, bullying, parental expectations, and societal expectations.

How to Ride the Peer Pressure Wave

Peer pressure is common, and you're definitely not new to this concept. As a teenager, peer pressure is a daily part of your life, and if you haven't already experienced it, you will soon enough. Peer pressure has a direct impact on your self-esteem. This is because you are pressured to fit in with the crowd, and if you don't, you might be bullied or made to feel like the odd one out. Besides having an impact on your self-esteem in this way, peer pressure is also related to self-esteem in the sense that if you have low self-esteem, you are more likely to fall prey to peer pressure (Schreiner, 2016).

With teenagers, peer pressure can take many different forms, such as the types of clothes that are acceptable to wear and all the types of music you should listen to. Peer pressure can also get dangerous because sometimes, your group of friends might force you to take part in activities that are risky and often could be considered minor criminal ones. The same goes for alcohol and substance abuse, as well as being involved in sexual activities that you might not be ready for.

Recognizing the Signs of Peer Pressure

As a parent, seeing the signs of peer pressure and recognizing them in your child can be the difference between making and breaking their self-esteem and also the path that their future will take. As a teenager, it is vital that you recognize the signs of peer pressure so that you do not get sucked into it. Knowing what the signs are will allow you to stop yourself once you realize you are being pressured by your peers, which will have a positive impact on your mental health and self-esteem. So, what are the signs, and what should you be looking out for as either a parent or teen? Woda (2014) describes the important signs that you don't want to miss:

- **Changes in behavior** are probably the most obvious sign. As a parent, the moment you notice that your teen is behaving differently than they usually do when they are in the company of certain friends, you need to pay closer attention. As a teenager, you might not notice this change for yourself, but your friends might. So, if one of your friends or family members points out that you are behaving differently, it might be a good idea to take some time to reflect, just in case it's the result of some peer pressure.

- You might feel like **you don't fit in**. As a teenager, it is normal to feel like you are different from your friends or the people around you. However, when you are being peer pressured, this feeling is intensified, and you become isolated or lonely. As a parent, this is a change that you need to watch out for.

- You might notice that your kid is **trying out new things**. While trying new things can be good sometimes, engaging in risky behavior is the one you need to look out for. For example, if your teen has never smoked before or tried alcohol but is doing that now, they are likely being peer pressured into doing it. It can just be your teen trying out new things, but it is always a good idea to get ahead of this in case there are more sinister aspects lurking about.

- If your teen is suddenly **obsessed with how they look** or their physical appearance, this could be a telling sign. This is especially true if they suddenly need a lot of branded clothing and expensive shoes, or if their sense of dressing changes drastically from what it used to be.

- One of the most common signs is that you're **doing things you don't actually want to do**. The moment you feel like you're not happy doing something, or you know in your mind that you don't want to do it, but your friends are forcing you to do it anyway, this is peer pressure. You might want to go ahead with carrying out the activity because you want to fit in, but of course, remember that it's just peer pressure.

- And lastly, another common sign is **poor performance in school**. Generally, kids who are being peer pressured tend to start having decreased grades. This could be because they are spending their time doing other activities or even because they don't want to seem intelligent because it's not "cool."

Do remember that these signs might be noticeable for many teenagers, but some people are so good at hiding them too. Just because your child is not displaying these signs does not mean that they are not experiencing this. It always helps to ensure that you are constantly having open conversations with your child so that they feel comfortable opening up to you if they are having any difficulties with peer pressure.

How to Cope With Peer Pressure

Being peer pressured is a difficult thing to go through, but just remember that you are not alone. You should always turn to your loved ones or people you trust when you feel that you are being pressured into doing anything you don't want to do. But if you're not yet ready to speak to someone, there are a few methods suggested by Pontz (2018) that you can use to deal with peer pressure:

1. Although you might desperately want to be part of the popular crowd or fit in, you need to have the courage to make the choice

and have the strength to act on your feelings and walk away. Find the strength in the knowledge that walking away might make you look like a fool in front of these people, but ultimately, you will have the self-esteem that they lack. You will be stronger for it.

2. Peer pressure doesn't always have to be negative. One way to avoid everything bad that comes from peer pressure is to find friends who have a positive influence on you. Try to surround yourself with people who have the ability to stand up to peer pressure because this will help you to stand up to it too.

3. Make sure you have limits and learn how to say no to people who are close to you. As a parent, it's important to teach your kid right from wrong so that they can identify when someone is telling them to do something that is morally incorrect. It's a good idea to teach them how to set their own limits, especially when it comes to things that make them uncomfortable.

4. Sometimes, the simplest solution is to completely avoid it. If you know a particular group of friends is always peer pressuring someone or the other, try to stay away from them. The best thing to do is to avoid associating with them so that they cannot force you to do anything you don't want to do. Remove yourself from those kinds of situations.

5. Being able to make decisions is another key factor in dealing with peer pressure. Learn how to make decisions for yourself and be confident in the knowledge that you are making the right choice. This will allow you to have a stronger mindset and will prevent you from being easily influenced by people who are trying to pressure you.

6. Making the consequences known to the group who are trying to force you to do something might help to reduce blood pressure. For example, if they are trying to get you to steal something from a convenience store, it might be a good idea to ask them if they've considered that everyone could go to jail if they do this activity.

7. Finally, one of the best ways for a teenager to deal with peer pressure is to talk to an adult. Of course, it needs to be an adult that you trust. As a parent, you need to let your child know that they can trust you and that you will be there for them in this difficult time.

Bullying and Self-Esteem

Bullying is an issue that has become so common in today's world that it seems almost normal. However, no child should have to go through this. The concept of bullying can be explained as "an act of harassment characterized by aggressive behavior, often involving a power imbalance between the bully and the bullied" (BetterHelp Editorial Team, 2023).

There are so many different types of bullying, and they can range anywhere from an act that barely has consequences to actions that have a massive effect on the victim and sometimes, even the bully. The BetterHelp Editorial Team (2023) briefly identifies four types of bullying: verbal, physical, social, and cyberbullying. With verbal bullying, as the name suggests, the bully often says nasty or mean things to the victim. Many times, it's simple name-calling, but it can also get extremely derogatory because it can escalate to threats and even sexual comments that make the victim uncomfortable or feel unsafe.

Physical bullying is any kind of harassment that has a physical effect on the person. This could be things like being beaten up, pushed or shoved around, and even sexual harassment. Then we have social bullying, which involves taking actions that impact the victim's social life. Being bullied in this way is often very embarrassing and can cause you to feel isolated because of false accusations or rumors. Finally, we have cyberbullying, which has picked up in recent decades with technology being so easily accessible.

This type of bullying takes place in the online world and can involve harassment on social media and any other online platform. Cyberbullying can encompass a broad range of harassment through fake posts on social media, comments that are hurtful or hateful, or even the creation of social media profiles with the purpose of pretending to be the victim to cause damage to their reputation.

Coping With Bullying: Identifying and Dealing With Your Bully

Bullying, of course, will have a detrimental effect on your self-esteem, but the first step to overcoming it is to learn how to identify a bully. Morris (2016) has found a few ways to easily help you identify a bully:

- One identifying characteristic of a bully is that they force themselves into your environment, whether it's physically or mentally.

- They speak to you in a way that makes you feel inferior.

- They have a way of making themselves seem like the victim, and you wind up looking like the bad guy.

- When they speak to you, the tone of their voice often does not correlate to what they're actually saying. For example, they might speak to you in a nice tone while saying hurtful things to you.

- They place a lot of effort into trying to control you in some way or the other.

- Bullies are extremely manipulative, and they will always get what they want from you, even if it means that they become aggressive and violent.

- You will have less energy when dealing with a bully. You will feel emotionally and physically exhausted, often doubting yourself because of them.

- They have a way of taking you away from all the people who care about you, which causes you to be isolated, and this makes it easier for them to bully you.

- Some of the more common points you will notice when you deal with a bully are that you're scared of them and that they are always threatening you. You don't look forward to seeing them at all, and most of the people around you don't like them.

Now that you know how to identify them, let's learn some important strategies on **how to deal with a bully**. Ohwovoriole (2022), a mental wellness expert, shares her tips for combating bullying:

- Most of the time, bullies harass you so they can continue the cycle of attacking you. That's why ignoring them and not engaging with them can be an effective tool.

- Underneath it all, bullies are just people who are also struggling with their lives, and sometimes, simply talking to them can help. Try speaking to your bully to see if the weight of how much they are harming you hasn't yet occurred to them. Sometimes, they may have personal issues that make them hurt other people. Of course, this doesn't always work, but in some instances, it might prompt the bully to get some help.

- It's always a good idea to take the issue to someone who can help, especially if you've tried talking to your bully, but it hasn't been resolved. You can report it to your teacher, parent, guardian, or anyone else that you trust.

It's not only by involving the bully in these resolutions that your problem can be solved. Sometimes, you need to take internal actions to deal with your bully. Here are some important strategies that Ohwovoriole (2022) shares:

- Combat all the negativity from your bully by remembering your positive affirmations. Remember everything positive, good, and that you love about yourself. Try to repeat them every day or write them out.

- Set your boundaries so that you can protect your space.

- Remember that it is never your fault that you are being bullied. A bully has their own mind, and they harm you because of their own troubles.

- Avoid changing your whole life to suit the bully's nature. Carry out your daily activities as you normally would and enjoy your life.

The only time that you should allow this to affect your life is if it is physically dangerous to you, and in this case, you will need some type of protection.

Thinking Points

Answer the simple questions below to help you recap, remember, and apply the important information you were introduced to in this chapter.

1. How does peer pressure impact a teenager's self-esteem?

2. What are the signs of peer pressure that both parents and teenagers need to be aware of?

3. What strategies can you use to cope with peer pressure?

4. How can bullying affect your self-esteem, and how can you identify a bully?

5. What are the different types of bullying, and what techniques can you use to deal with a bully?

6. Why is learning to stand your ground considered an important life skill, and how can you achieve this?

There are so many challenges surrounding peer pressure and bullying that will affect your life, shifting your perspective and altering your normal habits. This is when being able to stand your ground becomes a critical life skill. It is important to remember to apply the strategies you learned in this chapter to effectively fight this challenge.

Listening Up, Not Talking Down

Parenthood… It's about guiding the next generation, and forgiving the last. –Peter Krause (In A. Morin, These Parenting Quotes)

The relationship between a parent and child especially in the adolescent years is important because it is the "period of rapid biological, cognitive, and neurological changes" (Branje, 2018). It will have an effect on the way they function mentally and socially. Parents play a critical role in the development of their child's self-esteem too. This chapter will discuss what actions you, as a parent, can take to ensure that all your contributions to your teen's self-esteem are positive.

The Power of Parental Listening

According to Pickhardt (2019), it is one of the most important skills you can cultivate. It gives you the ability to truly pay attention to your kids and shows your interest in their lives. It gives your teen the perception that you will always have time for them and demonstrates your support. Your kid will feel validated and it encourages them to open up to you. Having regular open and honest conversations with your teens will teach them important skills and also equip them with the confidence they will need during these challenging teen years.

Topics like peer pressure and drug or alcohol abuse, as well as responsibility in various matters, are a good place to start (Agnihotri, 2023). You should also be conversing with them about topics related to their self-esteem, like how to set boundaries and develop healthy relationships (Agnihotri, 2023). Don't forget that this is not an opportunity for you to lecture your kids, but rather a chance to really listen to how they feel about these things and where they're facing challenges that you can help them with.

Strategies for Active Listening and Navigating Communication Breakdowns

Teenagers are probably some of the most difficult people to communicate with, and they can be pretty confusing too. One minute, you're having a great conversation and feeling so connected to them, but in the next, they're shutting down and telling you to go away. So, how do you navigate this? Here are a few tips outlined by Stanescu (2013) that will be incredibly helpful when dealing with communication breakdowns with your teen:

- **Parental control:** As parents, the need to constantly keep track of our kids can be overwhelming. But it can be challenging to navigate between hovering or overcaring and simply caring for their security. There are apps that you can use as a parent to keep track of your kids' whereabouts to make sure that they are okay and safe. However, when it comes to teenagers, this can be seen as invading their privacy and losing their freedom. It is important to ensure that you have a conversation with your teen about this so you can take steps to ensure their safety with their consent. Doing this will also show them that they can trust you, and they are less likely to go off on their own.

- **Misunderstandings:** Misunderstandings, especially in a social context, can happen very often. Parents generally don't understand the social media world in relation to their kids, and this is where cyberbullies take advantage. It is so important to ensure that you are monitoring your kids' social media usage. Again, you want this to be within reason and with their consent so that it does not create feelings of distrust and break down the communication between you and your children. If you are keeping track of their social media usage, you will be able to identify instances of cyberbullying, and you will be able to come to your child's rescue when needed.

- **Not understanding their friendship dynamics:** As a parent, it can be difficult to understand what goes on in the world of teen friendships, but it is important to be respectful of your teen's social groups and understand how they interact with each other before you can intervene so that you do not embarrass them when it is not necessary for you to even step in.

- **Giving them the time of day:** It is important to ensure that you aren't always rushed and appearing as if you have somewhere to be when you are interacting with your kids. If they feel like they are encroaching on your personal time or that they aren't being heard because you are in a hurry to get to some meeting, appointment, or anything else, they will put their walls up and will not want to communicate with you. You should always ensure that you have enough time to spend with your kids on other activities. This will give you the opportunity to bond with your kids in different settings and will help you improve their trust in you, which ultimately has a positive effect on communication.

There are a few other factors that influence whether or not your kid will communicate with you effectively, such as giving unsolicited advice, over or underreacting, and communicating nonverbally (Morris, 2019).

When it comes to advising them, your kid tends to shut down when you start to give them a sort of lecture whenever something happens. This is when you talk *at* them rather than *to* them. Most times, they just put up their walls and do not even listen to what you are saying, so it is important to make sure that you do not use this as an opportunity to begin blaming your kid or lecturing them for something.

When your kid comes to you with an issue, many times we end up overreacting. Sometimes, the issue might not be as big as it seems, and this makes our teens a little afraid to share things with us in the future. But there is an opposite to this too. Sometimes, when our kids tell us something, we don't react with as much emotion as they expect us to. If we want effective and open communication, and we want to prevent them from shutting down, we need to carefully consider our responses before reacting to them. Nonverbal messaging plays a huge role as well.

If we are having a conversation with our kids about something that they might be concerned with and our body language or facial expressions are not in line with the conversation or showing the kind of emotion that they want from us, this will cause a breakdown in communication. For example, if they are telling us about a case of bullying, and we have an expression of disgust instead of concern or empathy, they might feel like you don't really care, and might not want to share any future instances where they might be bullied, because they know that you don't really feel the emotions they expect you to feel.

All of these aspects go hand-in-hand and work together so you can achieve harmony in your communication with your child. Remember that there are repercussions if you allow yourself to let these communication barriers prevent proper open communication. Elliott (2022) explains that not communicating properly can cause a breakdown in the emotional bonding between you and your child. It can also cause issues with their behavior because they might become frustrated and start acting out.

It also affects you because you won't be able to understand your child's needs or what makes them stressed out, and eventually, this can also affect their behavior in school. They might become argumentative and aggressive in school. However, if you pay attention to these tips and strategies, you will be able to create the kind of safe space that you need for your child to be able to communicate with you openly and thrive.

Thinking Points

Answer the simple questions below to help you recap, remember, and apply the important information you were introduced to in this chapter.

1. Why is the relationship between a parent and a child during adolescence important, and how does it impact mental and social development?

2. What is the significance of parental listening, and can it contribute to a positive relationship with your teen?

3. What topics should be included during open and honest conversations?

4. What causes communication breakdowns, and what strategies can you use to navigate them?

5. What are the repercussions of not communicating properly with your teenager, and how can you combat this?

Now that you understand the importance of listening and validating your child's emotions and feelings, you are ready to learn how to help them out of the chaos. In the next and final chapter, you will learn how to help your teenager deal with stress in their life.

Guiding in the Chaos

The greatest weapon against stress is our ability to choose one thought over another. –
William James

The life of a teenager can be extremely chaotic, and it's important for parents to be able to guide them through this chaos. This chapter will discuss the role that you, as a parent, will play in helping your child navigate and deal with stress. You will learn some effective stress management techniques that you can teach your teenager to help them navigate the challenges that they experience. It will also help them to develop resilience, so they feel more empowered and stronger in their self-esteem.

Understanding Teenage Stress

Teenagers face an overwhelming amount of stress. Some of this is simply school pressures and others are related to their social environment. Either way, it is critical for parents to understand where the stress comes from so that they can be more supportive. Smith (2022) describes six stressors that your teen could be facing:

1. One of the most common stressors is in the academic field. It could be as simple as their test results or whether they're going to get into a good college.

2. Social stressors are also very common because teens often find themselves trying to fit in with the rest of their peers or social groups. Bullying and peer pressure can be extremely challenging for them too.

3. Family stressors play a role here too because if the family is facing any issues like parents who are going through a divorce or siblings who are bullying them, it can have a huge impact on their stress levels.

4. Events that happen around the world can stress out your teen too. Remember that kids who go to school are often exposed to the things that happen in this world daily, so when they hear about school shootings or any political events that cause unrest across the world, this can be traumatizing and stressful for them.

5. Anything that is traumatic, such as losing a friend or family member or loved ones who are ill, would have an impact on a teenager. Any type of abuse, whether mental, physical, or emotional, will also affect them negatively.

6. Lastly, any big life changes will cause stress. Some examples of this could be if they are relocating to a different city, changing schools, or going through any unusual changes in their family life such as divorcing parents.

Any of these factors can cause a devastating amount of damage to your teenagers' mental health, so it's important to teach them how to deal with these kinds of stressors. In the next section, we will explore the importance of emotional support, empathy, and validation, and the role that it plays to help teenagers cope with these fluctuating stress levels.

Emotional Support and Validation

As a parent, it's important to validate your child's emotions and acknowledge all of these things that have stressed them out. Mental Health First Aid USA (2021) outlines some very important strategies to assist you with being empathetic and using this to support your teen. The first way to do this is to ensure that you are listening without any harsh judgments. All you need to do here is let your teen speak without trying to pass any blame onto them or assuming what happened. Another technique is to ensure that you are listening intentionally so that you are paying the utmost attention to them without any distractions.

Doing this will make them feel validated and heard. If you have any previous ideas or thoughts on the issue that they are bringing to you, you need to ignore those assumptions and listen to your teen's point of view. Although you might think that relating your experiences to theirs might help, do not do this because it will invalidate their feelings, and they might feel as though they're being dismissed or ignored. Always remember to show them that you are okay with them feeling hurt or upset, and let it be known that you are there to support them no matter what.

Strategies to Teach Your Teen: Empathy and Stress Management

By now, you know that empathy is an important skill, but how can you equip your child with the empathy they need to handle their stress levels? (Austin, 2022):

- **You need to be the role model:** If a parent is able to incorporate empathetic behavior in their own lives and the way they communicate with their child, they will learn this behavior too.

- **Play devil's advocate:** This means that when your child is experiencing some kind of challenge, especially related to other people, you should be helping them to see things from that person's side too. This teaches them empathy and to see things from other people's perspectives.

- **Learning from history:** Teenagers are able to learn from historical mistakes. This means that they can look at how issues and conflicts were resolved in the past and understand things from the perspective of people back then.

Don't forget these next all-important stress management techniques. These will be the skills that your child should master because they will help them in their teenage years as well as for the rest of their lives.

The American Academy of Child & Adolescent Psychiatry (2019) explains the best ways to help your child navigate the stressors that drown them every day:

- Ensure that they are getting at least some good exercise every day and that they are eating proper meals. The meals should be balanced, healthy, and nutritious. It's very easy for teens who are under a lot of stress to completely forego their meals, but as a parent, you should keep an eye on this to ensure that they aren't losing out on vital nutrition.

- Sleep is key. It's so important to make sure that your kid is getting proper rest and relaxation so that their body and mind can recharge. Not having a proper sleep routine will increase their stress levels, because they will constantly be tired, and they will not be able to keep up with the demands of the day.

- Their caffeine intake needs to be limited because this increases the levels of cortisol in their body, which makes them more anxious and prone to panic attacks.

- You might have often heard people saying breathing can help reduce stress, and this is true. Breathing exercises can help your kid to relax. Teach them how to deep-breathe using their abdominal muscles. They can try meditation together with these deep breathing exercises, as this helps to reduce anxiety and can bring about a sense of calmness.

- You have already learned everything there is to know about negative self-talk in the earlier chapters, and it's important to remind your kids to implement this as a stress management technique too. They need to reduce their negative self-talk and turn it into a positive one.

- Teach them that it's okay to remove themselves from any stressful situation. They can do this by taking part in activities that help to calm them down, whether it is painting, journaling, running, or even spending time with a good friend or family member.

Thinking Points

Answer the simple questions below to help you recap, remember, and apply the important information you were introduced to in this chapter.

1. What are the common stressors that teenagers face, and how does understanding these contribute to better support for your teen?

2. What strategies can you use to provide support to your teen during times of stress?

3. How can you model empathetic behavior for your teen?

4. What stress management techniques can you use to teach your child to help them navigate daily stressors?

Remember that stress takes an incredible toll on your teen's self-esteem. Not managing stress appropriately can break them down, and it might be hard for them to recover. It can cause burnout and mental health issues such as depression and anxiety. You can use these techniques to help prevent this or treat it if your kid is already struggling with these issues. Yes, it can be challenging, but you've got this!

Conclusion

Put your heart, mind, and soul into even your smallest acts. This is the secret of success. —Swami Sivananda

Throughout all of the difficulties that your teen might face and the challenges that you will face as you help them on their journey to self-discovery and improved self-esteem, it is important to recognize and celebrate all of the accomplishments in your teen's life. It has such a positive impact and contributes to both the self-esteem and overall well-being of your teen. It's so easy to celebrate the small wins for your teen.

One of the best ways to do this is by praising them (Winlow, 2019). It's so encouraging when you tell them things like they've "done a good job" because they begin to feel like you appreciate them and this motivates them to become better. It also helps to boost their self-confidence. You can also reward them for anything that they do, such as artwork or a piece of journaling (Winlow, 2019). It doesn't even have to be extremely expensive; small rewards go a long way. There are so many ways to celebrate. Just remember to find the one that your kid responds to the most, the one that encourages them and makes them feel the most loved.

Remember to focus on everything good in your teen's life, and show them how to be grateful so that they can appreciate everything, which will contribute to a more positive outlook on their life. Show them how to be happy and celebrate their own wins too, so they can have a form of internal motivation and happiness with what they've done well. Take it one day at a time and remember to give yourself and your teen a break. Have a few self-care days when you kick back and relax, relieving the pressure off of you and your kid. Without them developing essential communication skills, they can never enjoy healthy relationships. Learning how to resolve conflicts, being more empathetic, and setting boundaries go a long way in the development of their self-esteem.

Now that you have all of this information, you are equipped with some of the best tools, techniques, and strategies to give your child the best life possible. You will be able to lighten their mental load and boost their self-esteem. You hold the key to their confidence and success in life. You are armed with some valuable insights and wisdom from this book, which prepares you and your teen to go on a journey of self-discovery and growth. The self-confidence you have gained will help you to navigate the challenges that your teen faces and will provide them with opportunities to grow and develop to become the best version of themselves.

By following the seven-step road map, you will discover the power of self-awareness, improving your self-love regardless of the beauty standards pushed onto you. Your self-compassion will improve, and your emotional resilience will be strengthened. You will experience the beauty of self-acceptance; loving yourself as you are. Your relationships will improve, and finally, you will have the strength to stand up for yourself no matter what challenges you face.

If you're a teenager who has come this far, it's time to claim your self-worth so you can venture out boldly into the world with the strength to conquer any challenges that dare to step in front of you. It is a tough journey, but it is a great one and at the end of it, you will emerge as a person you will be proud of. Using the seven-step roadmap to improve self-esteem, you can finally accept who you are, flaws and all. It's time to embrace the magnificence that is you, the brave, self-assured, and confident individual who has the world at their feet. Good luck on this incredible journey. We know we'll see you on the other side.

References

Accardi, J. (2019, September 27). *Help your child develop these 10 core components of self-esteem.* Advanced Psychology Services. https://www.psy-ed.com/wpblog/components-of-self-esteem/

Ackerman, C. (2018, November 6). *What is self-worth and how do we increase it?* PositivePsychology.com. https://positivepsychology.com/self-worth/

Agnihotri, A. (2023, July 19). Navigating adolescence: 7 essential conversations every parent must have with their teenager. *Hindustan Times.* https://www.hindustantimes.com/lifestyle/relationships/navigating-adolescence-7-essential-conversations-every-parent-must-have-with-their-teenager-101689769873690.html

Amaresan, S. (2019). *14 conflict resolution skills to use with your team and your customers.* Hubspot.com. https://blog.hubspot.com/service/conflict-resolution-skills

American Academy of Child & Adolescent Psychiatry. (2019). *Stress management and teens.* https://www.aacap.org/AACAP/Families_and_Youth/Facts_for_Families/FFF-Guide/Helping-Teenagers-With-Stress-066.aspx

American Psychiatric Association. (2019). *What is psychotherapy?* https://www.psychiatry.org/patients-families/psychotherapy

Andrade, S. (2021, July 1). *Council post: The importance of setting healthy boundaries.* Forbes. https://www.forbes.com/sites/forbescoachescouncil/2021/07/01/the-importance-of-setting-healthy-boundaries/?sh=4862faf856e4

Austin, A. (2022, June 13). *5 strategies for teaching empathy to teens.* Connections Academy. https://www.connectionsacademy.com/support/resources/article/teaching-empathy-to-teens/

Better Health Channel. *Relationships and communication.* (n.d.). Victoria Government. https://www.betterhealth.vic.gov.au/health/healthyliving/relationships-and-communication

BetterHelp Editorial Team. (2023, December 12). *The effects of bullying on a teen's mental health.* BetterHelp. https://www.betterhelp.com/advice/teenagers/the-effects-of-bullying-on-a-teens-mental-health/

BetterHelp Editorial Team. (2023, October 26). *12 reasons for developing greater emotional resilience.* BetterHelp. https://www.betterhelp.com/advice/resilience/12-reasons-for-developing-greater-emotional-resilience/

Blaine, J. (2020, November 29). *Self-concept and self-awareness.* Odyssey. https://odyssey.net.za/self-concept-and-self-awareness/

Branje, S. (2018). Development of parent-adolescent relationships: conflict interactions as a mechanism of change. *Child Development Perspectives, 12*(3), 171–176. https://doi.org/10.1111/cdep.12278

Canney, S. (2017, January 11). *5 important signs that you suffer from a distorted body image.* Women's Running. https://www.womensrunning.com/training/5-signs-suffer-distorted-body-image/

Carpenter, D. (2020, February 14). *3 ways to build real empathy for others in your life.* Verywell Mind. https://www.verywellmind.com/how-to-develop-empathy-in-relationships-1717547

Cherry, K. (2022, November 7). *What exactly is self-esteem?* Verywell Mind. https://www.verywellmind.com/what-is-self-esteem-2795868

The Children's Society. (2021). *What is emotional resilience?* https://www.childrenssociety.org.uk/information/young-people/well-being/resources/emotional-resilience

Dugan, R. (2021, October 11). *6 reasons it's important to embrace your imperfections.* LinkedIn. https://www.linkedin.com/pulse/6-reasons-its-important-embrace-your-imperfections-rosemary-dugan

Elliott, C. (2022, April 23). *The overlooked (but potentially devastating) effects of not talking to your kids*. Somocom Lab. https://www.somocomlab.com/post/the-overlooked-but-potentially-devastating-effects-of-not-talking-to-your-kids

Emerson, R. W. (n.d.). *Ralph Waldo Emerson quotes*. Goodreads. https://www.goodreads.com/quotes/876-to-be-yourself-in-a-world-that-is-constantly-trying

Empowered Teens and Parents. (2016, May 16). *Self-esteem quiz for teens from My feet aren't ugly, self esteem work book*. https://empoweredteensandparents.com/self-esteem-quiz-for-teens-from-my-feet-arent-ugly-self-esteem-work-book/

Fran. (2022, April 25). *What is a growth mindset and how can you develop one?* FutureLearn. https://www.futurelearn.com/info/blog/general/develop-growth-mindset

Frew, H. (2021, January 20). *7 factors influencing your body image*. Counselling Directory. https://www.counselling-directory.org.uk/memberarticles/7-factors-influencing-your-body-image

Galindo, P. M. (2021, April 30). *What is gratitude? 5 ways to be thankful*. BetterUp. https://www.betterup.com/blog/gratitude-definition-how-to-practice

Gur, T. (2023, May 21). *Never bend your head. Always hold it high. Look the world straight in the eye - Helen Keller*. Elevate Society. https://elevatesociety.com/never-bend-your-head-always/

Healthdirect Australia. (2019, November 10). *Self-talk*. Australian Government. https://www.healthdirect.gov.au/self-talk

Herrity, J. (2019). *How to write smart goals (with examples)*. Indeed. https://www.indeed.com/career-advice/career-development/how-to-write-smart-goals

Indo Asian News Service. (2019, September 28). Positive social relationships help shape, boost self-esteem. Here's how. *Hindustan Times*. https://www.hindustantimes.com/sex-and-relationships/positive-social-relationships-help-shape-boost-self-esteem-here-s-how/story-tsAuPHYTMxzB4WWwyZ7bZO.html

Israel, I., & Madden, H. (2023, November 12). *11 ways to embrace your flaws and imperfections.* WikiHow. https://www.wikihow.com/Embrace-Your-Flaws

James, W. (n.d.). *William James quote.* Goodreads. https://www.goodreads.com/quotes/120416-the-greatest-weapon-against-stress-is-our-ability-to-choose

Kuttappa, D. S. (2022, February 8). *Self-acceptance: significance and ways to enrich it.* Medium. https://shoury01.medium.com/self-acceptance-significance-and-ways-to-enrich-it-caedf23a6b31

Lawler, M. (2022, February 2). Body image: definition, how it affects health and well-being, and when it's a problem. EverydayHealth.com. https://www.everydayhealth.com/body-image/

Liles, M. (2022, October 10). *101 uplifting confidence quotes for days you're struggling with low self-esteem.* Parade. https://parade.com/989608/marynliles/confidence-quotes/

Martin, S. (2017, January 30). *16 quotes to inspire healthy relationships.* PsychCentral. https://psychcentral.com/blog/imperfect/2017/01/16-quotes-to-inspire-healthy-relationships#Quotes-to-Inspire-Healthy-Relationships

McElroy, M. (2015, November 2). *Children's self-esteem already established by age 5, new study finds.* UW News. https://www.washington.edu/news/2015/11/02/childrens-self-esteem-already-established-by-age-5-new-study-finds/

McGinley, K. (2017, June 22). *5 ways to embrace imperfection.* Chopra. https://chopra.com/articles/5-ways-to-embrace-imperfection

Mental Health First Aid USA. (2021, August 23). *Practicing empathy as a mental health first aider.* https://www.mentalhealthfirstaid.org/2021/08/practicing-empathy-as-a-mental-health-first-aider/

Mind. (2022). *About self-esteem.* https://www.mind.org.uk/information-support/types-of-mental-health-problems/self-esteem/about-self-esteem/

Moore, M. (2022, September 8). *Here's 3 ways boundaries can help you.* PsychCentral. https://psychcentral.com/relationships/the-importance-of-personal-boundaries

Morgan, P. (n.d.). *Dozens of famous and powerful resilience quotes | author, keynote speaker & workshop leader.* Solutions for Resilience. https://www.solutionsforresilience.com/resilience-quotes/

Morin, A. (2022, November 2). *These parenting quotes will help you keep things in perspective.* Verywell Family. https://www.verywellfamily.com/inspirational-parenting-quotes-1094736

Morris, J. (2016, March 10). *14 ways to identify a bully.* Watersedge Counselling. https://watersedgecounselling.com/14-ways-to-identify-a-bully/

Morris, K. (2019, April 3). *Three common barriers to communication with your teen.* Campbell County Health. https://www.cchwyo.org/news/2019/april/three-common-barriers-to-communication-with-your/

Murrihy, C. (2022, September 21). *How to spot the early signs of negative body image.* ISPCC. https://www.ispcc.ie/early-signs-of-negative-body-image/

MyTutor for Parents. (n.d.). *4 steps to help your teen overcome setbacks.* https://www.mytutor.co.uk/blog/parents/4-steps-to-help-your-teen-overcome-setbacks/

Nash, J. (2018, January 5). *How to set healthy boundaries & build positive relationships.* Positive Psychology. https://positivepsychology.com/great-self-care-setting-healthy-boundaries/

Neff, K. (2019). *Definition and three elements of self-compassion.* Self-Compassion. https://self-compassion.org/the-three-elements-of-self-compassion-2/

Nixon, R. (2011, May 15). *The neuroscience of self-esteem, self-criticism and self-compassion.* Livescience.com. https://www.livescience.com/14151-neuroscience-esteem-criticism-compassion.html

Norton, F. (2018, January 2). *Self-confidence: The golden key to your life success.*Www.linkedin.com. https://www.linkedin.com/pulse/self-confidence-golden-key-your-life-success-fred-nyirongo-1

Nurhawa, N. (2023, June 25). *The role of empathy in personal and professional relationships.* Medium. https://medium.com/@nurisetianur/the-role-of-empathy-in-personal-and-professional-relationships-ec24623d02e

Ohwovoriole, T. (2022, January 24). *What to do if you're the victim of bullying.* Verywell Mind. https://www.verywellmind.com/how-to-deal-with-bullies-5213915

Olympia Benefits. (2021, September 28). *Causes of negative self-talk and how to overcome It.* https://www.olympiabenefits.com/blog/causes-of-negative-self-talk-and-how-to-overcome-it

Perera, K. (2020, May 28). *The importance of self-acceptance.* More Self Esteem. https://more-selfesteem.com/more-self-esteem/building-self-esteem/the-significance-of-self-acceptance/

Perry, E. (2022a, September 14). *What is self-awareness, and why is it important?* BetterUp. https://www.betterup.com/blog/what-is-self-awareness

Perry, E. (2022b, December 21). *Self-reflection: Learn how to better understand yourself.* BetterUp. https://www.betterup.com/blog/self-reflection

Pickhardt, C. E. (2019, April 15). *The power of parental listening to their adolescent.* Psychology Today. https://www.psychologytoday.com/us/blog/surviving-your-childs-adolescence/201904/the-power-parental-listening-their-adolescent

Pompa, R. N. (2011, May 15). *The neuroscience of self-esteem, self-criticism and self-compassion.* Livescience.com. https://www.livescience.com/14151-neuroscience-esteem-criticism-compassion.html

Pontz, E. (2018, September 4). *Peer pressure: Strategies to help teens handle it effectively*. Center for Parent and Teen Communication. https://parentandteen.com/handle-peer-pressure/

Pradeepa, S. (2022, October 19). *20 famous people with a growth mindset*. Believe In Mind. https://www.believeinmind.com/self-growth/famous-people-with-a-growth-mindset/

Quora. (n.d.-a). *What are the most popular stories of people who overcame their low self esteem to become successful?* https://www.quora.com/what-are-the-most-popular-stories-of-people-who-overcame-their-low-self-esteem-to-become-successful

Quora. (n.d.-b). *What are the most popular stories of people who overcame their low self esteem to become successful?* https://www.quora.com/what-are-the-most-popular-stories-of-people-who-overcame-their-low-self-esteem-to-become-successful

Rainne, S. (2020, July 20). *How to say no and assert your boundaries*. Supportiv. https://www.supportiv.com/healing/how-to-know-your-boundaries-assert-yourself#6

Raypole, C. (2019, December 13). *Healthy relationships: 32 signs, tips, red flags, and more*. Healthline. https://www.healthline.com/health/healthy-relationship

Raypole, C. (2021, May 17). *Ready, set, journal! 64 journaling prompts for self-discovery*. PsychCentral. https://psychcentral.com/blog/ready-set-journal-64-journaling-prompts-for-self-discovery#takeaway

Roberts, E. (2015, October 23). *Practicing self-compassion increases your self-esteem*. HealthyPlace. https://www.healthyplace.com/blogs/buildingselfesteem/2015/10/practicing-self-compassion-can-increase-self-esteem

Saeed, M. (2023, June 12). *Embracing authenticity: Overcoming psychological barriers to self-acceptance*. LinkedIn. https://www.linkedin.com/pulse/embracing-authenticity-overcoming-psychological-barriers-marina-saeed

Saraswati, S. (n.d.). *Sivananda Saraswati quote*. Goodreads. https://www.goodreads.com/quotes/113425-put-your-heart-mind-intellect-and-soul-even-to-your

Schreiner, M. (2016, October 7). *Peer pressure and low self-esteem*. Evolution Counseling. https://evolutioncounseling.com/peer-pressure-and-low-self-esteem/

Scott, E. (2022, May 24). *The toxic effects of negative self-talk*. Verywell Mind. https://www.verywellmind.com/negative-self-talk-and-how-it-affects-us-4161304

Smith, K. (2022, October 21). *6 common triggers of teen stress*. Psycom. https://www.psycom.net/common-triggers-teen-stress

Smith, V. C. (n.d.). *18 quotes to inspire self-kindness and self-compassion*. Hope+Wellness. https://www.hope-wellness.com/blog/18-quotes-to-inspire-self-kindness-and-self-compassion

Stanborough, R. J. (2020, November 25). *Negative body image: Definition, causes, symptoms, treatment*. Healthline. https://www.healthline.com/health/negative-body-image

Stanescu, B. (2013, July 4). *Five barriers to parent-child communication: Bridging gaps with parental control*. Bitdefender. https://www.bitdefender.com/blog/hotforsecurity/five-barriers-to-parent-child-communication-bridging-gaps-with-parental-control/

Ulrich, S., & Paulson, D. (2021, August 9). *Promoting healthy body image*. Mayo Clinic Health System. https://www.mayoclinichealthsystem.org/hometown-health/speaking-of-health/promoting-healthy-body-image-in-children-teens

Vadlamani, S. (n.d.). *Embrace imperfection: Six ways to celebrate your flaws*. Happiness.com. https://www.happiness.com/magazine/personal-growth/embrace-your-imperfections/

Vanessa. (2019, November 10). *Body positive quotes for better body image*. Live Simply Natural. https://livesimplynatural.com/body-positive-quotes-for-better-body-image/

von Goethe, J. W. (n.d.). *Johann Wolfgang von Goethe quote*. Goodreads. https://www.goodreads.com/quotes/18941-as-soon-as-you-trust-yourself-you-will-know-how

Waters, B. (2013, May 21). *10 traits of emotionally resilient people*. Psychology Today. https://www.psychologytoday.com/intl/blog/design-your-path/201305/10-traits-emotionally-resilient-people

Watson, S. (2021a). *Oxytocin: The love hormone*. Harvard Health Publishing, Harvard Medical School. https://www.health.harvard.edu/mind-and-mood/oxytocin-the-love-hormone

Watson, S. (2021b, July 20). *Dopamine: The pathway to pleasure*. Harvard Health Publishing, Harvard Medical School. https://www.health.harvard.edu/mind-and-mood/dopamine-the-pathway-to-pleasure

Weber State University. (n.d.). *Self-esteem*. https://www.weber.edu/counselingcenter/self-esteem.html

Winlow, C. (2019, July 31). *5 simple ways to celebrate your child's accomplishments and achievements*. Red Kite Days. https://redkitedays.co.uk/5-simple-ways-celebrate-childs-accomplishments-achievements/

Woda, S. (2014). *7 obvious signs your teen is suffering from peer pressure*. uKnowKids. https://resources.uknowkids.com/blog/7-obvious-signs-your-teen-is-suffering-from-peer-pressure

Wooll, M. (2021, July 26). *A growth mindset is a must-have — These 13 tips will grow yours*. BetterUp. https://www.betterup.com/blog/growth-mindset

youth.gov. (2011). *Characteristics of healthy & unhealthy relationships*. https://youth.gov/youth-topics/teen-dating-violence/characteristics

Yung, C. G. (n.d.). *C. G. Yung quote*. Goodreads. https://www.goodreads.com/quotes/39433-your-visions-will-become-clear-only-when-you-can-look

Zitz, S. (2023, February 13). *Get inspired with these 100 empowering self-love quotes*. Prevention. https://www.prevention.com/life/a42827694/self-love-quotes/